Reducing the Burden on the Poor

CERC Monograph Series No.2

Reducing the Burden on the Poor

Household Costs of Basic Education in Gansu, China

Mark BRAY
DING Xiaohao
HUANG Ping

Comparative Education Research Centre
The University of Hong Kong

Gansu Basic Education Project

First published 2004
Reprinted 2006 by

Comparative Education Research Centre
Faculty of Education
The University of Hong Kong
Pokfulam Road, Hong Kong, China

In collaboration with the Gansu Basic Education Project

© 2004 Cambridge Education Consultants (CEC) and
Gansu Provincial Education Department (GPED)

ISBN 962 8093 32 0

Cover design by Vincent Lee

Layout by Emily Mang

Contents

List of Abbreviations

CEC	Cambridge Education Consultants
DFID	Department for International Development
GBEP	Gansu Basic Education Project
PA	Participatory Approaches
PCE	Potential Cost of Education
PMO	Project Management Office
SDP	School Development Planning
UBE	Universal Basic Education
UK	United Kingdom
UNESCO	United Nations Educational Scientific & Cultural Organisation
UNICEF	United Nations Children's Fund

List of Tables

List of Figures

List of Boxes

Maps of China, Gansu and four project counties

Units of Measurement
1.00 yuan = approximately 0.12 US dollars
1.00 mu = 0.16 acres or 0.07 hectares

Foreword

The achievements of the Gansu Basic Education Project (GBEP) have attracted attention both nationally and internationally. The project was designed to pilot a number of different education initiatives in poor minority areas. One of the key strategies for increasing access of poor students has been to reduce the financial burden on poor parents. The GBEP has piloted six new approaches in this area, including scholarships, budgetary reform and free lunches.

In order to assess the effect of these initiatives, the GBEP commissioned an independent review. The findings of this review, which are presented in this book, summarise the experience of these pilots, analyse which initiatives have been most successful, and record some of the lessons learned in the process of implementation. The review was conducted at a time when China's rural education tax system was undergoing reform. It was therefore able not only to help the GBEP project plan for the future, but also to highlight key aspects of education financing which are of interest to national and international audiences.

I thank every student, teacher, official and consultant who contributed to the review, and congratulate them on their achievement. I also thank the Review Team, led by Professor Mark Bray, for producing an accessible introduction to the GBEP experience.

Li Weiguo

Project Director, Gansu Basic Education Project (GBEP)
Vice Director, Gansu Provincial Education Department

Introduction

This publication presents findings by the three authors, working as a team, following their investigation of dimensions of the costs of education in parts of Gansu Province, China. It mainly focuses on the four counties served by the Gansu Basic Education Project (GBEP), which was launched in 1999 and funded by the Department for International Development (DFID) of the United Kingdom government. Initially the GBEP had a five-year lifespan, but in 2002 it was extended by a year and the budget expanded to UK£12.2 million (158.6 million yuan). The GBEP is widely recognised to have had a major impact on basic education in Gansu, and to some extent has provided a model for others to follow, both in China and in other countries. This study focuses on one part of the GBEP from which instructive lessons can be learned.

The GBEP was launched in the context of the government's Open the West policy and the drive to achieve universal basic education in China by 2010. This had long been a national goal, and had already been achieved in many parts of the country. In some regions, however, some children still did not enrol in school; and of the ones that did enrol, many dropped out. This pattern was particularly prominent in areas

Figure 1: GBEP Project Structure

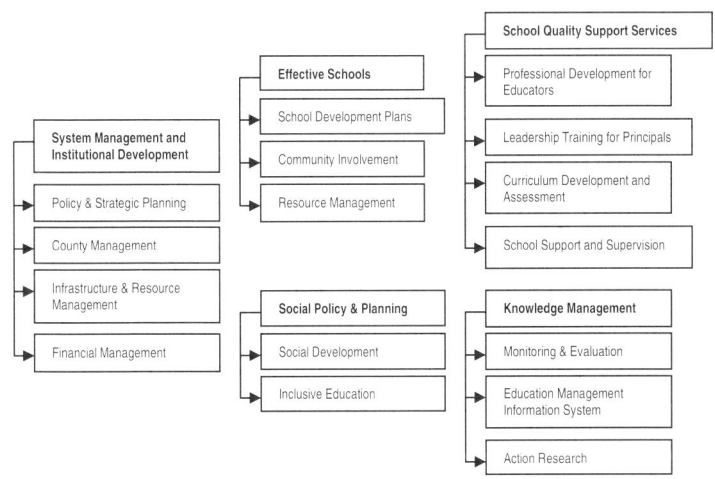

inhabited by ethnic minorities, including various parts of Gansu Province. Within the main GBEP objective of increasing enrolment in poor minority areas, the project has a particular focus on girls. The GBEP particularly focuses on primary schooling, but also has project inputs for junior secondary schooling. Inputs are concentrated on four counties in Linxia Autonomous Prefecture of Gansu Province: Kangle, Hezheng, Dongxiang and Jishishan. The GBEP project structure is shown in Figure 1.

Many schools are in remote mountain areas

This study focuses on the range and effectiveness of initiatives piloted by GBEP to reduce the costs of schooling to households. It examines both financial and other costs, including opportunity costs. The household costs of schooling have major implications for enrolment and retention in school. When the costs are too high, children either never attend school at all or drop out at an early stage. The study notes the magnitude of the burden on household budgets, observing variations according to geographic location, occupation and other factors.

Household costs are of course not the only determinant of whether children enrol and stay in school. Many other factors must be considered, including sickness, disability, distance, curriculum and general attitudes towards schooling. The people who designed the GBEP and who are implementing it are well aware of these factors. This study enhances the clarity with which issues may be perceived, and presents case studies which highlight the circumstances and attitudes of a range of families in different locations and socio-economic strata. Experience from elsewhere in China and from other parts of the world (see e.g. Asian Development Bank 2001; Bruns et al. 2003; Hannum 2003) shows that no single strategy will succeed in overcoming all these obstacles. Continued effort will be needed to tackle different constraints in different ways.

Within the GBEP, the six components which are particularly relevant to this study are:

- a budgetary arrangement at the government level known as the two commitments,
- a scholarship scheme for poor children,
- boarding allowances for junior middle school girls,
- a textbook revolving fund,
- a free-lunch programme, and
- energy-saving buildings.

Since some of these components are more complex than others and have different implications, the six components are given different amounts of space in this study. Much of the analysis may have relevance to other projects which will in the future be undertaken by DFID and by other agencies, not only in China but also in other parts of the world.

Challenges, Achievements and Structures in the Education System

Demographically, China is a multiethnic society in which 92 per cent of the population are Han Chinese and most of the rest comprise 55 officially-recognised ethnic minorities (Postiglione 1999). Less than 30 per cent of the population live in urban areas, and over 70 per cent live in rural, mountainous or remote areas (Law 2000, p.355). Part of the challenge for education is to cater for diversity while providing a unifying framework for the nation as a whole.

When compared with other countries of similar economic levels, China has long stood out as having enrolment rates that are relatively high (Lee 2002, pp.65-69). To a large extent this has been the result of persistent efforts by the central, provincial and local governments during the decades since 1949 (Han 1990). In 1986 the Sixth National People's Congress sought to consolidate achievements and provide the mandate for further progress by passing a law on compulsory education (China 1986). Article 2 proclaimed that:

> The state shall institute a system of nine-year compulsory education. The authorities of provinces, of autonomous regions, and of municipalities directly under the Central Government shall decide on measures to achieve compulsory education, in the light of the degree of economic and cultural development in their own localities.

This directive was operationalised in different ways in different parts of the country. In 1995, the State Council (quoted in China 2000, p.9) indicated that universalisation of nine-year compulsory education meant that:

> the enrollment rate of primary school-aged children will reach at least 99% by the year 2000. And the gross enrollment rate of school age children at the lower secondary stage will reach 85% or so, and the goal of universalizing 9-year compulsory schooling will be attained in areas inhabited by 85% of the nation's population. In poor areas inhabited by 10% of the nation's population, main efforts will first be directed toward making 5-6 year primary schooling universal, and in extremely poor areas inhabited by 5% of the nation's population, main efforts will first be directed toward making 3-4 year primary schooling universal.

Parts of Linxia Autonomous Prefecture of Gansu Province, in which the GBEP operates, were among the extremely poor areas, and gained special attention.

The structure of the school system varies in different parts of the country. As noted in one official document (China 2000, p.29), in areas where the entire length of primary and lower secondary education is nine years, there exist three parallel systems: a 6+3 system, a 5+4 system, and a nine-year integrated system. In areas where the entire length is eight years, 5+3 is the dominant system. Most of the primary schools served by the GBEP are on a five-year system, after which pupils who proceed to lower secondary schools are in a three-year system.

Also relevant to the present study is the system of teaching points. These are junior primary schools, usually going up to Grade 3 but in some cases going up to Grade 4. The teaching points are all in remote areas, and help reduce the distance that children must travel each day from their homes. Pupils who reach the top classes in teaching points must transfer to primary schools to continue their education. Because by this stage the pupils are older, they generally find the extra travelling distance less burdensome than they would otherwise.

Within the schools and teaching points, most teachers are public employees on standard conditions of service and are known as *gong ban* teachers. A few, however, are described as temporary employees and are known as *dai ke* teachers. For some of these teachers, 'temporary' may be an extended period lasting for several years or longer. Most *dai ke* teachers have low qualifications, but many are dedicated and are especially important in remote areas which cannot easily recruit *gong ban* teachers. Also, since *dai ke* teachers earn much lower salaries, they cost considerably less.

The problem of financing of basic education in China, as in other parts of the world, is a difficult task for the authorities. The government would like to be able to provide education that is completely free of charge throughout the stage of compulsory education, but finds that in

Eager to study

practice it is necessary for schools to charge fees to cover at least some costs. Some schools charge a range of fees to cover specific items, such as textbooks, stationery and examinations, in addition to general school fees and class fees. Most schools in the counties covered by the GBEP are grouped into school zones. In most cases government regulations set ceilings for fees, but within that ceiling decisions on the nature and scale of fees may be made either by individual schools or by zones.

Social Contexts and Attitudes to Schooling

During the first year of the GBEP, a Baseline Survey was conducted. It showed that the populations and per capita incomes of the four counties covered by the GBEP were fairly similar in magnitude (Table 1). Also, all counties have significant minority populations. However, the counties have important differences; and variations are also evident within the counties. Thus, within individual counties some parts are more prosperous than others; and some communities, even in fairly close proximity, are entirely Han while others are entirely minority.

Table 1: Populations and Incomes in the Four Counties (2001)

County	Population	% minority in population	Average rural per capita income (yuan)	% of population below poverty line
Dongxiang	250,000	80 (mostly Dongxiang)	706	28
Hezheng	186,400	48 (mostly Hui)	872	17
Jishishan	218,000	50 (Baoan, Hui, Tibetan, Sala, Tu, Dongxiang)	752	26
Kangle	229,000	55 (mostly Hui)	885	9

Source: GBEP Document 33 (2001), Table 2.1.1.

Especially in resource-constrained settings, the motives for sending or not sending children to school tend to be a mix of economic and social. Economic motivations relate to perceived short-term and long-term rates of return (see e.g. Mehrotra & Delamonica 1998; Bray 2002; Deininger 2003). Few households would express this to themselves or others in a mathematical way. However, many households do make rough assessments of the costs of schooling and of the alternative uses that could be made of the resources, including time and labour, that would have to be devoted to schooling (Penrose 1998; Boyle et al. 2002; Bray 2003). Such alternative uses of time and labour could include care of younger children by older ones, tending of animals, general house-work, and work on agricultural plots.

Social motivations are to a large extent shaped by the attitudes and actions of peers and higher-status individuals in the community. When enrolment rates are low, households which do not send their children to school tend not to be considered unusual. However, when enrolment rates exceed a threshold after which households which do not send their children to school are a small minority, then social pressure on those households helps to raise enrolment rates towards univer-salisation (Williams 1983; DFID 2001; UNESCO 2001). This type of social pressure from peers, combined with pressure from the govern-ment and other agencies, is clearly raising enrolment rates in the four counties. However, the pressure has not yet proven adequate to achieve full universalisation.

In the cultures of the four counties, two specific social factors which are related to each other require particular attention. One is the role of religion, and the other is the general attitude towards schooling of girls. Under the heading of religion, the impact of Islam is especially relevant (Gladney 1999). The Muslim communities in the four counties share social structures and attitudes with many other parts of the Islamic world. Particularly in low-income Islamic communities, it is common to find that much stronger emphasis is placed on the education of boys than of girls, and in some settings the education of girls is actively discouraged. In some societies, such as Indonesia or Malaysia, at the level of primary education this pattern has been changed so that universal education for both genders has basically been achieved (UNESCO 2000); but in other societies, such as northern Nigeria, Pakistan and Yemen, it remains the case that boys are much more likely to be enrolled in school than girls (Hyde 2001; UNESCO 2002).

This matter is of course a function of other cultural factors in addition to religion, and gender disparities are common in non-Islamic low-income countries as well as in Islamic ones (Colclough et al. 2000; UNESCO 2003). In many cases, the reasoning by householders is partly linked to perceptions of the purposes of schooling. If schooling is expected to lead to cash-earning employment, it is widely argued, then boys are more likely than girls to seek such opportunities and to benefit from the necessary investment. Girls, by contrast, may be expected to marry at a young age and then to be involved in domestic activities which have less need for the sorts of skills provided by school systems (Gertler & Glewwe 1991; Ma & Zheng 2003). When the girls become women, and then marry and leave to serve another family, their parents may feel that their investments have been lost. In some societies, girls are described as transient outsiders, guests or someone else's property, like "water spilled out" or a "bird in the courtyard", and "a commodity on which money is lost" (Croll 2001, p.234). Box 1 provides an example from one head of household in Gansu who was interviewed by the authors and who did not consider schooling of girls to be an investment deserving priority amidst competing claims on his resources. In some settings, moreover, schooling may seem to have a negative effect which 'spoils' girls by encouraging attitudes which do not fit with prevailing social norms (see e.g. Hyde 2001; Lee 2002). Also, since schooling occupies a significant amount of time each day, it can obstruct pupils from learning skills in housework, childcare and agriculture which will be needed in their adult life.

The GBEP has particular focus on girls

Nevertheless, while the portraits presented above may have some general applicability, considerable variation arises within individual households and communities. In the domain of religion, much depends on the attitude and demonstration effects of religious leaders. While some Islamic leaders in the four counties frown on the education of girls, others actively encourage such education on the grounds that it can help to strengthen the communities. Project personnel have tried to identify local-level change agents and then to work with them to expand enrolment rates.

Box 1: Available Resources, but Other Priorities

All the 200 teaching points in the four GBEP project counties are located in rural areas. One, which is in many respects typical, is situated on a hillside overlooking a valley which at the time of the researchers' visit in July was bursting with ripening crops. This particular teaching point dates its history back to 1962.

The teaching point has strong brick buildings, two of which were constructed by the GBEP, and is surrounded by a wall. Next door is the original pair of school buildings, which have been converted into a private residence for Mr Ma and his family. Mr Ma originally lived on the land now occupied by the school. He took the old school buildings and land in exchange for releasing his land for the new construction.

The main room of Mr Ma's house, converted from a classroom, is not luxurious but is comfortable and clean. It is supplied with electricity, and in the centre is a good stove. Along the sides are a bed, chairs, and a table with a radio, and taking pride of place is a golden clock with a swinging pendulum.

What was once the school playground is now a well-swept farmyard. Hay is stacked in one corner next to a trailer, and chickens peck on the ground. In the second classroom block, one room houses a sheep and the other has been converted into a barn with shovels, sickles and other agricultural equipment. Mr Ma has 17 mu (1.2 hectares) of land nearby.

Mr Ma has three children: a son aged 10 and two daughters aged nine and six. The son attends the school next door, and is supported by a GBEP scholarship. But the daughters do not go to school. "We are too poor," explains Mr Ma. "We cannot afford it."

While Mr Ma is certainly not rich, his claim of poverty is not entirely convincing. Further, his family background makes his situation perhaps a little surprising. A certificate on the wall of Mr Ma's front room announces that his father had been granted official permission to practise as a medical worker. With some pride, Mr Ma explains that although his father had only schooled up to Grade 3, he had gained a profession for himself. However, adds Mr Ma, "I was the eldest son and was unable to go to school because I had to look after my younger brother and two sisters".

Mr Ma then reveals that his younger brother not only gained some schooling, but became a *dai ke* teacher in the school next door. When asked whether the brother would like his two nieces to attend school, Mr Ma replied that indeed he would. "But we are too poor", he repeated.

This family is indeed aware of the cost of schooling. With only slight exaggeration, Mr Ma indicated that it requires 200 yuan a year to send a child to school. He knows this from the expenses for his son, which include not only the fees but also pencils, a school bag and other necessities. In the case of his son, half of the cost is paid by the scholarship even though Mr Ma's family is clearly not among the poorest in the village.

Mr Ma says that if he received scholarships for his daughters, he would send them to school too. This might indeed be the case; but many families

(continued on next page)

(continued from previous page)

which are much poorer than Mr Ma's succeed in sending their daughters to school. It seems that the real reason why Mr Ma does not send his daughters is that he has other priorities. He simply does not consider education of his daughters to be a worthwhile use for his money.

The final irony of this situation is a relic from the buildings' former existence as a school. Emblazoned across the wall of the barn, opposite Mr Ma's front door, is a slogan in large white characters. "Study hard, and become educated!", it exhorts. Yet in Mr Ma's family, only his 10-year-old son is able to read it.

Government Expenditures on Education

In 2001, Wang Shanmai and his assistants conducted a study commissioned by the GBEP on costs to governments and households in the four counties plus Linxia County (Wang 2001). The team collected data on operating expenses per student in rural areas from official sources (Table 2). Some of the operating expenses were met from per-pupil fees, so the costs to the governments were defined as comprising these operating expenses minus the income from fees. In all counties, the operating expenses per student were higher at the secondary than at the primary level. This was to be expected, since secondary teachers generally have higher salaries than their primary school counterparts, and secondary schools also have greater needs for equipment. However, the gap between the two sets of figures varied considerably in different counties, presumably reflecting factors such as variations in class sizes. Operating expenses per primary school student were considerably higher in Dongxiang than in the other counties, but the expenses per secondary school student were recorded as lowest in Dongxiang. Wang's

Table 2: Operating Expenses per Student in Rural Primary and Secondary Schools, by County, 2000 (Yuan)

	Kangle	Hezheng	Dongxiang	Jishishan	Linxia	Average
Primary	257	246	428	270	334	327
Secondary	752	547	487	786	550	624

Source: Annual Education Finance Report of Education Commission, in Wang (2001), p.7.

report did not explain the reasons for these patterns; and it did not comment either on the definition of 'rural' and the consistency of the application of the definition, or on the extent to which the official figures could be considered reliable. Nevertheless, the statistics are a useful indicator of government expenditures on education.

Table 3 presents additional data collected by the present authors on revenues for primary and secondary education in two of the project counties in 2002, and compares them with national figures for the nine-year rural compulsory education in 2001. Budgetary education revenues in Hezheng and Kangle accounted respectively for 72.9 and 76.5 per cent of total revenues for education, with the balance being made up from social donations, institutional revenues and other sources. Institutional revenues formed a much lower percentage of total revenues in the two counties than across the country in the nine-year rural compulsory education allocation. This reflected the poverty of the two counties and thus the limited capacity to raise income from fees. Nevertheless, as shown below, other figures collected by Wang (2001) indicated that the burden on households was considerable.

A 2001 World Bank provincial expenditure review contained a chapter on education which presented data from two of the four GBEP counties, namely Hezheng and Jishishan (World Bank 2001). It highlighted the existence of various grants for education, including the central government's "state-designated poor areas compulsory education project" grant. Hezheng had passed the Universal Primary Education (UPE) inspection in 2000, but Jishishan had not yet passed the inspection and thus continued to receive significant resources from this grant. However, the report also indicated that the system suffered from over-decentralisation. The result of responsibility for the provision of basic education being pushed to the level of townships, and sometimes even villages, was too heavy a financial and management burden for those levels of government. Expenditures on personnel formed a particularly high proportion of the total in those two counties, representing 98.3 per cent in Hezheng and 93.4 per cent in Jishishan in 1999, compared with 83.2 per cent for the whole of Gansu.

Table 3: Educational Revenues in Hezheng and Kangle Counties, 2002 ('000 Yuan)

	---- Hezheng ----		---- Kangle ----		National allocation for 9-year rural compulsory education, 2001
	Amount	%	Amount	%	%
Total	23,429	100.0	30,119	100.0	100.0
I. Fiscal Educational Revenues	17,089	72.9	23,044	76.5	
of which: Budgetary Educational Revenues	17,089	72.9	23,044	76.5	70.4
Surcharge collected by governments					9.3
II. Social organisation and individual-run school revenues					1.1
III. Social Donations	2,340	10.0	3,736	12.4	2.8
IV. Institutional Revenues	1,740	7.4	1,487	4.9	13.5
of which: student fees	1,069	4.6	1,487	4.9	10.2
V. Others	2,260	9.6	1,852	6.1	2.0

Source: Hezheng and Kangle Annual Finance Statistics, 2002; China Education Annual Finance Statistics, 2002.

The Nature and Scale of Household Costs

Direct Costs

Table 4 presents data on the fees charged by schools in Wang's sample. The data were calculated on the basis of the fees charged by the schools rather than on the actual expenditures of students, and in practice not all students paid all fees. For the students that did pay, however, the figures represented the lowest direct household cost per child for one year of schooling.

Comparing the data shown in Tables 2 and 4, Wang concluded that most of the operating costs per student were met by the government (Table 5). However, the proportions were markedly different at primary and junior middle levels. The average proportion was 74.1 per cent at the

Table 4: Fees Charged by Primary and Junior Middle Schools, by County, 2000 (Yuan)

| County | Level | Total Fees | Misc. Fees | Other Fees | | |
				Subtotal	Textbooks	Stationery	Others*
Kangle	Primary	134	13	121	70	37	14
	Junior middle	329	30	299	225	27	47
Hezheng	Primary	114	10	104	80	20	4
	Junior middle	310	20	290	235	20	35
Dongxiang	Primary	91	16	75	49	21	5
	Junior middle	294	24	270	232	26	12
Jishishan	Primary	127	15	112	90	20	2
	Junior middle	344	20	324	214	40	70
Linxia	Primary	101	10	91	62	25	4
	Junior middle	246	20	226	182	34	10
Average	Primary	110	13	97	65	26	6
	Junior middle	301	23	278	216	29	33

Note: The data are on the basis of fees per student charged by all schools. In practice, however, the fees varied by grade; and not all students paid all the fees in full.

* 'Others' includes class fees, insurance fees, heating fees in winter, and test-paper fees.

Source: Wang (2001), p.8.

the primary level, ranging from 66.7 to 81.9 per cent in the five counties. At the junior middle level, the average proportion was 66.6 per cent, ranging from 61.2 to 69.0 per cent. In other words, households appeared to bear between a quarter and a third of the operating costs of primary education, and about a third of the costs of junior middle education.

Because the fees for textbooks are usually the largest component of the direct costs on households, the present authors investigated that matter in more detail. The national government has a policy to provide free textbooks:

- for all students in rural areas where five or six years of primary education has not been universalised, and
- economically-needy junior middle students in rural areas where nine years of education has not been universalised.

Table 5: Proportions of Operating Costs met by Government and Households, by County, 2000

		--Government--		--Household--	
	Cost per student	Amount (yuan)	%	Amount (yuan)	%
Primary					
Kangle	478	344	72.0	134	28.0
Hezhang	350	236	67.4	114	32.6
Dongxiang	503	412	81.9	91	18.1
Jishishan	382	255	66.7	127	33.3
Linxia	425	324	76.2	101	23.8
Average	424	314	74.1	110	25.9
Secondary					
Kangle	1,051	722	68.7	329	31.3
Hezhang	837	527	63.0	310	37.0
Dongxiang	757	463	61.2	294	38.8
Jishishan	1,110	766	69.0	344	31.0
Linxia	776	530	68.3	246	31.7
Average	902	601	66.6	301	33.4

Source: Wang (2001), pp.8-9.

Among the four project counties, Dongxiang and Jishishan were eligible for the first of these categories during 2002/03, and all four counties were eligible for the second. However, the way that the policy had been implemented meant that some burdens remained. One problem was that financial allocations to schools to enable them to provide the textbooks free of charge had been fixed according to the enrolments in 1999. Because of enrolment increases, some schools had had to spread the financial allocations rather thinly. For example, the students in Sanhe Teaching Point in Jishishan only enjoyed allocations of 10 yuan each rather than the 18 yuan to which they had apparently been entitled under the policy.

Further, Dongxiang and Jishishan had been requested by Gansu Provincial Government to pass the examination of universal primary education by the end of 2002/03. If and when this task is accomplished – either on paper or in reality – the subsidies may cease to be available from the national government. Table 6 shows that the burden which would no longer be met by the national government is considerable. If and when the counties subsequently pass the threshold for junior middle education, the burden will be increased further.

Table 6: Cost of the Primary School Free Textbooks Policy

Grade	Autumn semester of 2002 (yuan per student)	Spring semester of 2003 (yuan per student)	Number of books per student	Jishishan County		Dongxiang County	
				Student number	*Cost*	*Student number*	*Cost*
1	22.80	18.00	6	8,169	147,042	9,692	164,764
2	23.60	19.70	6	5,399	106,360	5,102	93,111
3	27.80	19.00	6	4,537	86,203	4,243	62,372
4	27.50	20.15	7	3,488	70,283	3,474	74,170
5	28.60	23.45	7	2,360	55,342	2,829	60,541
6*	28.30	23.3.0	7			831	19,362
Total				23,953	465,230	26,171	474,320

* Some schools were on five-year cycles while others were on six-year cycles.
Source: Official document about free textbooks issued by Gansu Provincial Government, 2003.

The ways that the costs of textbooks translated into fees per student varied. According to national policies for rural compulsory education in poor areas, in 2002 annual fees set by schools to cover textbooks and other costs could not exceed to 160 yuan at the primary level and 260 yuan at the junior middle level. However, this policy was not strictly adhered to; and both between and within counties were some instructive variations.

The authorities in Dongxiang County had a policy which differentiated between rich, middle-income and poor areas in the county, and which set the ceiling on fees which schools in those areas were permitted to charge. The policy was designed to protect children from poor households, though one side-effect was that children in middle-income and rich areas could gain better-resourced education and therefore that inequalities were maintained. The maximum fees permitted under this policy are set out in Table 7. This framework was distinctive to Dongxiang, and the other project counties did not report a comparable policy which differentiated by area.

Table 7: Maximum Fees Permitted in Dongxiang County, 2002/03 (Yuan per Student per Semester)

	Rich areas	Middle-income areas	Poor areas
Primary	60	40	30
Junior middle	180	160	120

Source: Officials in Dongxiang County, 2003.

The ways in which policies on fees were or were not translated at the school level may be illustrated by some examples. Table 8 shows data on seven schools visited by the authors of this study. In all schools the fees increased at higher grades; and in one school the fees in all grades (which should be multiplied by two to show annual fees) exceeded the limits set by national policy. Whereas three schools just set overall fees, the other four provided breakdowns. The component for textbooks varied to an extent which might at first sight seem surprising given that all schools followed the same national curriculum and acquired the standard books from branches of the same company. The variations can partly be explained by the fact that some schools had more demanding requirements for exercise books than other schools, and partly that some schools required students to purchase full sets of books rather than just the core books. Since the funds for free textbooks were not available in time in the last semester, students had to pay for textbooks in advance. In order to reduce family burdens, some schools did not require students to purchase books in music, art, etc.; and whereas some schools purchased black-and-white books, others opted for colour.

Nevertheless, in all cases the fees were very transparent, and in one school they were announced on a board on an exterior classroom wall close to the main entrance. Gongbeiwan Teaching Point was distinctive in its policy of only charging fees for boys and not for girls. Sixteen of the 35 girls received GBEP scholarships, so the remaining 19 girls were in effect given scholarships by the school/community.

Table 8: Fees in Selected Schools, per Semester, 2002/03 (Yuan)

	Beizhuangwan Primary (Dongxiang)	Gongbeiwan Teaching Point (Dongxiang)	Xiaoguan Primary (Jishishan)	Baizang Primary (Jishishan)	Taizijie Primary (Hezheng)	Zhangmajia Teaching Point (Hezheng)	Gaolouzi Primary (Kangle)
Grade 1	25	25 boys only (girls no charge)	55	55	textbook 47.7 notebook 8.0 exam paper 3.0 magazines 5.3 school fee 15.0 class fee 3.0 *Total 82.0*	textbook 38.0 notebook 1.5 school fee 15.0 *Total 54.5*	textbook 14.3 notebook 2.0 school fee 15.0 *Total 31.3*
Grade 2	25	27 boys only (girls no charge)	60	65	textbook 49.5 notebook 8.0 exam paper 3.0 magazines 5.5 school fee 15.0 class fee 3.0 *Total 84.0*	textbook 40.0 notebook 1.5 school fee 15.0 *Total 56.4*	textbook 16.1 notebook 2.0 school fee 15.0 *Total 33.1*
Grade 3	30	30 boys only (girls no charge)	75	65	textbook 65.3 notebook 13.0 exam paper 4.0 magazines 6.5 school fee 15.0 class fee 3.0 *Total 106.8*	textbook 50.0 notebook 5.0 school fee 15.0 *Total 70.0*	textbook 36.7 notebook 5.0 school fee 15.0 *Total 53.7*
Grade 4	30		80	textbook 44 notebook 9 exam paper 1 school fee 13 class fee 3 *Total 70*	textbook 75.0 notebook 13.0 exam paper 4.0 magazines 6.5 school fee 15.0 class fee 3.0 *Total 116.5*	textbook 50.0 notebook 5.0 school fee 15.0 *Total 70.0*	textbook 35.2 notebook 5.0 school fee 15.0 *Total 52.2*
Grade 5	30		80	textbook 44 notebook 9 exam paper 1 school fee 13 class fee 3 *Total 70*	textbook 68.8 notebook 13.0 exam paper 5.0 magazines 6.5 school fee 15.0 class fee 3.0 *Total 111.3*		textbook 38.7 notebook 5.0 school fee 15.0 *Total 55.7*

Note: Gongbeiwan Teaching Point only had classes up to Grade 3, and Zhangmajia Teaching Point only had them up to Grade 4.

Concerning actual payment of the fees, not all schools had complete records; and among those that did have good records, different practices were evident in the matter of partial payment. In one school, it appeared from the records that pupils either paid the whole fee or none at all, while another school accepted partial payments. Good record-keeping is important not only for general clarity but also to protect the teachers from accusations of embezzlement. In practice, at least some teachers, rather than taking money, have contributed part of their salaries to their schools; but in the absence of clear records, it is impossible to know how much they have contributed or to ensure that they are appropriately reimbursed when funds become available.

The practice of accepting non-payment, partial payment or delayed payment of fees is also a way in which schools recognise that households may have more cash in some seasons than in others. Poor households in particular are only able to pay school fees after the harvest season. This is a major reason why many households find it easier to pay fees for the first semester of the academic year than for the second semester. All teachers claimed that they do allow students to remain in school even without payment of fees, though no doubt occasions do occur in which teachers push out pupils. On the other side, there is always the possibility that pupils might refuse to pay fees on the grounds that they hope for a scholarship, but the authors did not find any evidence of this happening. The most problematic pattern is when pupils themselves withdraw from school because of perceived pressure (even when that pressure is not necessarily great) and because of shame. This is a general phenomenon in poor communities, and was also evident in the four counties in Gansu.

In addition to the fees, households had to meet other costs of schooling. Since most rural children walked to school, they did not incur transportation costs. Also, none of the schools sampled required students to wear uniforms. However, the schools did expect students to purchase bags, pencils and other stationery. These demands could add up to 20 yuan or more per annum, with amounts increasing in the higher grades.

Returning to the data presented by Wang (2001), it is useful to note his calculations of the balance between household expenditures on education and household total expenditures. Many households could only raise money for education by going into debt (Box 2). Typical ways to do this were to borrow from relatives or friends (Table 9), which allowed the households to have expenditures which exceeded their net incomes.

Table 9: How Households Raise Money for Education, by County, 2001

		Average	Kangle	Hezheng	Dongxiang	Jishishan	Linxia
All expenditure	%	66.3	70.6	70.3	47.1	40.0	100.0
from household income	Yuan	372	304	404	337	429	356
Borrowing from	%	22.5	11.8	13.4	41.2	45.0	0
relatives or friends	Yuan	62	9	29	77	166	0
Other (including	%	14.6	17.6	20.0	14.5	15.0	0
donations, bank loans and arrears)	Yuan	16	15	60	35	21	0

Source: Wang (2001), p.12.

Elaborating on this picture, Table 10 presents figures calculated by Wang for the five counties covered by his survey on the potential cost of education borne by households and the proportion that this potential cost forms out of total expenditures and net incomes. The potential cost of education represents Wang's estimate of the lowest cost of education to households when all children of school-age are enrolled, and combines the cost of primary and junior middle education. Net income refers to total income, including in-kind income, minus the costs of production such as seeds and fertilisers. The table shows that on average for the five counties, the potential cost of education represented 12.2 per cent of total household expenditures and 24.9 per cent of net incomes. These figures are artificial insofar as they represent what the costs would be if all children enrolled in school, when in practice all children do not enrol. Nevertheless, they can be placed alongside other data collected by Wang on the economic burden of schooling of the children who do attend school; and together the sets of indicators are instructive measures.

Wang then proceeded to show the differences between low-income and high-income households, and to correlate these figures with dropout rates. The ratio of the potential cost of education to household net incomes was 6.6 per cent for the richest quartile of income groups, 14.2 per cent for the next quartile, 22.6 per cent for the third quartile, and 47.1 per cent for the poorest quartile. As might be expected, these figures were closely correlated with dropout rates: the poorer the household, the greater the economic burden and the greater the likelihood of children dropping out.

Table 10: Ratio of Potential Household Cost of Education to Total Expenditures and Net Incomes, by County, 2001

	Average	Kangle	Hezheng	Dongxiang	Jishishan	Linxia
Potential cost of education (PCE) (yuan)	404	451	487	441	388	279
PCE as % of total household expenditures	12.2	16.4	13.4	10.5	12.1	8.4
PCE as % of household net incomes	24.9	35.2	21.7	17.8	31.5	15.3

Source: Wang (2001), p.11.

The GBEP has significantly raised enrolment rates

Box 2: Going into Debt for Education

The Deng family live in a rural part of Jishishan County. The family consists of Mr Deng (aged 52), his mother (aged 79), his wife (aged 46), and three children. The oldest child, a son, is aged 19 and is in the first year of Lanzhou Minority College. The middle child is a daughter aged 15 and in the first year of middle school, and the youngest is a daughter aged eight in Grade 1 of the local teaching point.

The fact that all three children are in full-time education must be considered a major achievement for the Deng family. It is only achieved with considerable strain, however, and is plunging the family into debt. The costs this year are much more than last year, when the oldest child was only in middle school, the second one was still in primary, and the youngest had not yet set foot on the ladder.

The family owns 6 mu of land, which can usually provide enough grains and vegetables for household consumption. Last year the harvest was good, and Mr Deng was able to earn 400 yuan from sale of beans and vegetable oil seeds. When there is a drought, however, the family has to secure food from relatives. The family has also borrowed three sheep from relatives, hoping that the sheep will bear lambs and thus pay for themselves. A lamb could sell for approximately 200 yuan. Last year, Mr Deng also worked for two months in Qinghai Province as a labourer. His income was 780 yuan, but after paying his expenses he could only bring home 400 yuan. He tried to supplement his income by collecting plants for traditional medicine, but found that his earnings did not even cover the costs of transportation.

The biggest expenditure is for the son's education. Fees in the college are 5,000 yuan a year, and living costs are about 2,000 yuan a year. The costs for the second child have greatly increased now that she is in junior middle school. The school is far from home, and so she needs to board. She did win a 50 yuan scholarship from the European Union; but that is only a small contribution to the total costs, which exceed 900 yuan a year. The third child benefits from the GBEP free-lunch programme, but was not deemed eligible for a scholarship. Her school fees are 66 yuan a year, and about 30 yuan is needed for stationery and other consumables.

Mr Deng of course also has other pressing needs. He must pay 48 yuan a year in agricultural taxes, and requires fertilisers costing 300 yuan for his fields. In addition, his mother and other family members need medicines costing about 540 yuan, and another 130 yuan is needed for general consumables.

To pay for all this, Mr Deng has this year gone heavily into debt. He has borrowed 500 yuan from a local credit fund, 4,500 yuan from relatives, 2,150 yuan from friends, and 400 yuan from the middle school head teachers. "I am really worried," sighed Mr Deng. "It's all very well to say that my son will in due course find a job; but it's not so easy to find a job these days, and anyway I have to wait till he graduates. I have really no idea how I can repay all these debts."

Opportunity Costs

The literature on opportunity costs shows that the concept is complex and that measurement is difficult (see e.g. Bray 1996a; Tsang 1997; Boyle et al. 2002). Concerning the opportunity costs to households, Wang (2001, p.12) distinguished between what he called Type 1 and Type 2 opportunity costs as follows:

- *Type 1* costs are the loss of income from a child's schooling. The loss arises because the child cannot work elsewhere when the child is in school or is travelling to/from school.
- *Type 2* costs are the lost utility from the fact that expenditures on fees and other school-related items cannot be deployed to other uses. Such uses could be for consumption or for invest- ment.

Type 1 opportunity costs are a function not only of the hours that children devote to schooling, but also of the labour market and the nature of home production. The value of labour generally becomes greater as children get older.

Concerning the GBEP project counties, Wang (2001, p.12) used children's main activities after dropping out as an indicator to reflect the influence of Type 1 opportunity costs on schooling. He observed that relatively few primary-school-aged dropouts engaged in farming or outside work, but that the proportion increased significantly for the junior-middle age group. He added that most dropouts helped their families with agricultural planting, but that since this was a seasonal activity the out-of-school children were underemployed. Also, there were few wage-earning employment opportunities in the region, and the interviewed families had little expectation of finding jobs. On this basis, Wang considered the Type 1 opportunity costs to be low.

Nevertheless, the costs can be significant in some families. Inter- viewees for the present study indicated that opportunity costs are not only a matter of planting and paid labour: they can also be a matter of herding animals. If one sheep can be sold for 250 to 300 yuan, and if a child can look after three to five sheep, even over a period of a year the child can help the family to earn well over 1,000 yuan. Also, some families earn significant income through trading (Box 3). A parallel sociological study of one village in Ningxia Province has noted that none of the children of the richest family attended school because they all helped their parents with business in the township (Zhou et al. 2003).

Type 2 opportunity cost is a relative concept which reflects how a family values investment in human capital as opposed to investment in physical capital or consumption, and may play a more important role in schooling. Wang (2001, p.13) took the Type 2 opportunity cost of education for one primary school child at 110 yuan, and noted what other uses could have been made of that money. This sum, he observed, was equivalent to the wheat output of half a mu of land or to six months' grain ration for an adult. At junior middle level, the Type 2 opportunity cost was taken as 301 yuan, i.e. nearly three times the amount for primary schooling. The Type 2 opportunity cost for a primary student could cover fertilisers sufficient for four mu of wheat and pesticides for 20 mu. Wang's questionnaire and interview data showed that many families could not afford sufficient fertilisers and pesticides. Therefore, Wang concluded (p.13), the agricultural yields of these families would have been larger if they had not invested in schooling.

An additional observation links ethnicity and family size. Both types of opportunity cost increase with the number of children in the family; and, partly because official policy permits them to do so, minority families tend to have more children than Han families. This factor suggests that opportunity costs for minority families are greater than for Han families.

Concerning gender, Type 1 opportunity costs are likely to be greater for boys than for girls since boys are more likely to seek wage-earning employment. However, girls can also undertake agricultural and even wage-earning work; and they are more likely than boys to be assigned domestic duties, such as looking after younger siblings, which can release adults for external work. Type 2 opportunity costs would seem to be more gender neutral, since the alternative uses for the money would be the same wherever the money came from. However, as observed above, the relative value that parents place on investment in schooling compared with investment in other uses is likely to vary by gender.

Box 3: The Opportunity Costs of Schooling

The Xie family hails from a village in Dongxiang County, but now keeps residences both there and in Lanzhou, the provincial capital. The village house is managed by the grandparents, while the parents and their children stay in Lanzhou where the younger Mr Xie runs a small shop.

The younger Mr Xie and his wife have been resident in Lanzhou for some time, but were joined by their sons only last year. Until that point, the boys were attending school in Dongxiang. The elder reached junior middle school and the younger reached Grade 4, but both have now dropped out in order to help their parents with the business.

The grandparents have some regrets that that the children left school, but they observe that the costs of schooling are much higher in Lanzhou than in Dongxiang. Moreover, adds the elder Mr Xie, "my son and daughter-in-law need the children to help in the shop." Though the grandparents do not know how much their son and his wife earn in Lanzhou, they consider it very worthwhile for the children to help with the business. While the children were in the village, their parents had to send over 1,000 yuan each year for their education, but since the boys went to Lanzhou only 300 yuan has been sent back to the village. "The boys help the family earn at least a few thousand yuan each year," the grandfather said.

Compared with others in the village, this family is relatively wealthy. The grandparents have a colour TV, and their house was recently decorated. "Everything was done by our son," declared the grandmother proudly.

When asked about the future education of their grandchildren, both grandparents laughed. "Of course, the boys should continue if they can study well and if their parents do not need them at the shop. But the reality is that they are needed for the business; and anyway, the elder boy has some junior middle school education while the younger one has done most of the primary cycle. That's already a lot more than many other children in the village."

These grandparents clearly think that in the balance between keeping children in school or asking them to help with the family shop, their son and daughter-in-law have made the right decision. Their only major regret is that the family are not resident in the village. The grandparents hope that in a few years' time they will join the younger generations in Lanzhou.

Specific Project Components

This section of the study focuses in turn on six specific project components of the GBEP which directly affect the financial burden on households. The last part of the section adds comments on some other components which have an indirect relationship.

The purpose of GBEP is to increase enrolment in poor minority areas – thereby helping achieve Universal Basic Education (UBE) – and to reduce the inequalities which exist in the education system. Figure 2 shows the conceptual framework through which the GBEP aims to transform the operation of schools. The GBEP has six project outputs, the second of which is:

> ➤ *Output 2*: Increased participation by poor and disadvantaged children, girls and minority groups.

One of the activities for achieving this output is:

> ➤ *Activity*: Methods of reducing the direct costs of, and charges for, education designed and piloted before the end of 2004 and success evaluated

This is the framework within which the project has experimented on reducing costs of schooling for the poor households.

Within the GBEP, the six pilots which are particularly relevant to this study are:

- a budgetary arrangement at the government level known as the Two Commitments,
- a scholarship scheme for poor children,
- boarding allowances for junior middle school girls,
- a textbook revolving fund,
- a free-lunch programme, and
- energy-saving buildings.

Figure 2: Framework for Transformation of Schools through the GBEP

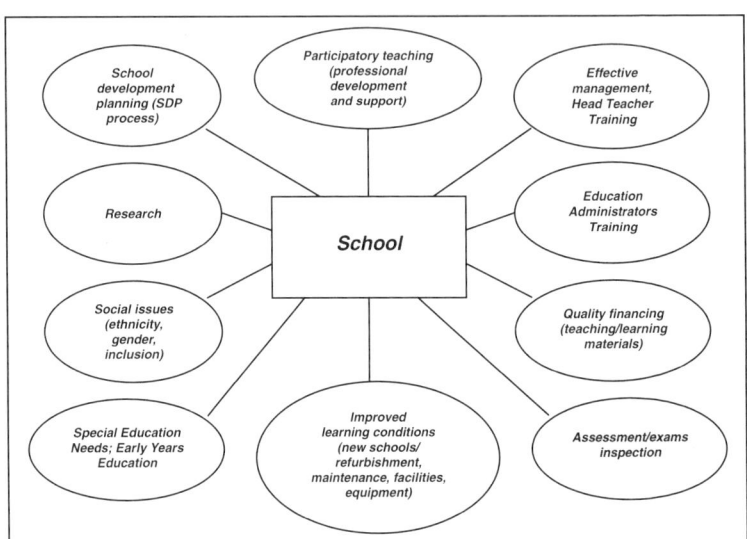

The Two Commitments

The architects of the GBEP were mindful that many achievements of externally-funded projects collapse as soon as the external funds cease to be available because the necessary mechanisms for local resources to phase in as external resources phase out have not been put in place. In Gansu a particular problem was that inadequate government resources had previously been made available to education, particularly for components other than teachers' salaries, and there was a danger that after the project the situation would revert to its former state. The Two Commitments were designed to address this issue. The initial project documents set out the basic concepts, which were refined in the first year (GBEP Document 16, 2000). The Two Commitments are:

1. County budgetary allocations to education (excluding matching grants for the national government's Compulsory Education Pro-

ject) in county fiscal expenditures will increase by 1 percentage point every year.

2. The percentage share of county budgetary allocations to non-personnel expenditures, and expenditures on student financial aid (excluding matching grants required by state and provincial budgets) in recurrent educational expenditures from county budgetary allocation (i.e. excluding grants from educational authorities at upper-level governments) will increase by 1 percentage point every year in two counties, and by half a percentage point every year in the other two counties.

The national government has a similar policy which is entitled the Three Increases. This policy was first enunciated in the 1985 Decision by the Central Committee of the Communist Party of China on the Reform of the Educational Structure (China 1985, p.5), and subsequently incorporated into the 1986 Law on Compulsory Education (China 1986, Articles 12 and 14). The Three Increases are that:

1. The growth rate of budgetary allocations for education made by the central and local governments should be higher than the growth rate of recurrent financial revenues.

2. Per student recurrent educational expenditures and per student expenditures on non-personnel expenses (called public expenses in Chinese terminology) should increase each year.

3. Teachers' salaries should increase each year.

Compared with the Three Increases, the Two Commitments are more detailed and impose a stricter financial requirement on the county governments. In addition, a detailed formula has been agreed with each county to determine the distribution of funds to schools (with higher relative weightings given to more remote schools). This formula is directly linked to the plans schools make for the future through the School Development Planning process (see Appendix).

The Two Commitments have considerable significance not only in the four GBEP counties but also more widely. In 1993, the national government embarked on a reform of the system of taxation, requiring provincial governments to give more money to the central government. The move was intended to restore the balance of power between the central government, which had become weaker, and the provincial governments, which had become stronger. In the meantime, according to the Implementation Suggestions of the State Council on the Guidelines for the Reform and Development of Education in China, issued in 1994, the central government has the policy-making and overall planning role for education but implementation is left to local governments. The provinces have the overall responsibility for formulating the development plan for basic education, and for providing assistance to counties to help them to meet recurrent expenditures in education. The responsibility for actually implementing compulsory education in rural areas lies with the counties; and in practice the responsibility lies with townships and villages.

Partly because of the taxation reform, however, for several years it was rare for schools to receive recurrent non-personnel funds from county governments because financial capability of local governments had been significantly weakened. As a result, schools found that they had to impose fees on students to pay for almost everything except teachers' salaries. Usually, incomes at the school level were insufficient to meet needs. The Two Commitments push the governments of the GBEP project counties to allocate more priority to education when they make budgets, and in particular to give schools in the four counties additional money to cover their recurrent non-personnel expenses. In turn, this should reduce the need for schools to charge fees, thereby reducing the burden on households. Schools in other counties of Gansu Province are said to be envious of this situation, and school-level personnel in the four GBEP counties greatly value the fact that the Two Commitments are part of the project.

As is common with such matters, however, gaps exist between official policy and actual implementation. The ways that the Two Commitments were implemented during the initial years of the GBEP varied in different counties. For 2002 and 2003, every county did have detailed budget figures on money from the second commitment, including lists which showed the allocations to each school. Distribution was said to be based on weighted factors for poverty, low enrolment, type of school, etc., and the system thus appeared to be a major advance in both equity and transparency. Documents showed that in 2002 and 2003 the county governments transferred money to the school districts, after which each school should have received reimbursement based on the budget for its prepaid expenditure.

Nevertheless, as in all parts of the world some bodies are more influential than others. Wang's (2002a) study of overall budgetary allocations for education in the project counties showed a tendency for bodies which were geographically closer to the decision-makers and which in other ways had stronger political connections to gain larger allocations than their less influential counterparts. As might be expected, variations also occurred in the smoothness of operation in different counties. Specifically on the second commitment, Table 11 which shows completion rates of the budget in 2002, indicates a range from 62.4 per cent to 101.4 per cent.

Table 11: Implementation of the Second Commitment, 2002 ('000 Yuan)

	Dongxiang	Jishishan	Hezheng	Kangle
Non personnel expense budget (A)	98.4	114.5	64.7	52.9
in which: Amount of 1999 (A1)	58.2	70.0	22.0	8.0
Scholarship (A2)	3.5	3.4	5.4	7.8
Distribute to schools (A3)	36.7	41.1	37.3	37.1
Completion of (A)	98.9	70+44 = 114.5	-	33
	100.0%	99.6%		62.4%
Completion of (A1)	58.2			
Completion Rate	100.0%			
Completion of (A2)	3.5			
Completion Rate	100.0%			
Completion of (A3)	37.2			
Completion Rate	101.4%			

Notes:

1. In contrast to other counties, in Jishishan the Finance Bureau rather than the Education Bureau directly allocates money to schools, and the Education Bureau does not know the exact situation. For execution of the Two Commitments, the Education Bureau was given 440,000 yuan while the Finance Bureau allocated the other 700,000 yuan as non-personnel expenditures for education.

2. The accountant in the Hezheng Education Bureau stated that the execution rate of the Two Commitments in his county was 100%, but he did not confirm it with detailed figures and his statement did not match the audit report. One informant stated that the audit report for 2002 was not detailed, and that it only mentioned that "completions of the Two Commitments in Hezheng and Kangle were not good".

Source: County-level accountants.

Also important to note is that, despite the efforts to clarify matters at an early stage in the project, definitions of the Two Commitments differed among the counties. For example, the Dongxiang budget in the base year (1999) was quite large because it included a subsidy for teachers' household heat in winter which would normally be considered a personnel expenditure. Such variations in starting points are among the additional reasons for variations in implementation.

Further transparency and effectiveness in the system can be promoted by clear understanding at the school level of how the system works. When headteachers were asked by the authors of this study how the Two Commitments policy could help their schools to get more money for non-personnel uses, none could explain clearly about the distribution criteria (Table 12). In most cases there was a gap between the budget allocations and the amounts actually received by schools.

As in many projects, personnel changes posed further threats to implementation. In Kangle, the officer who had signed the document agreeing to the Two Commitments had left his post in 2002, and the head of the Finance Bureau had left the position in 2003. Education personnel feared on the one hand that the replacement officers might not understand the Two Commitments policy and mechanisms as clearly as their predecessors, and on the other hand that the newcomers might be less committed to the concepts behind the scheme. In addition, further training and support seems to be needed for financial managers at all levels.

A further complication arose from a taxation reform launched in all project counties in 2002 which aimed to reduce the financial burden on peasants. This was part of ongoing evolution of mechanisms and strategies at the national level (Tsang & Ding 2003; Wang et al. 2003). In Kangle, for example, peasants were relieved of the levy of five yuan per person for rural education. In Linxia Prefecture as a whole, the income from the levy had been 8-10 million yuan in 2001, but this loss was more than compensated for by inter-governmental transfers of 42 million yuan in 2002 of which 36 million yuan was used for education. Within the education allocation, 19.6 million yuan had been allocated to a fund for upgrading school buildings and 16 million to teachers' salaries, demonstrating the low priority attached to quality improvement.

Table 12: Comparison of Budget Allocations with Receipts Reported by School Heads

	2002 budget	Receipts reported by school head	2003 budget	Remarks by school heads
Dongxiang				
Beizhuangwan Primary	1,620	520	3,095	The standards of non-personnel expenses are: - (8 yuan/month *gong ban* teacher, 5 yuan/month *dai ke* teacher) = 8 x 4 (*gong ban* teachers) x 12 (months) - expense for heating: 200 yuan/year
Gongbeiwan Teaching Point	1,620	500	1,748	The standards of non-personnel expenses are: - 2 teachers have 120 yuan = 5 x 2 (*dai ke* teachers) x 12 = 120; - 35 per class x 3 classes = 105 - others: 120 - heating: 40 per class x 3 classes = 120, 60 per teacher x 2 = 120
Jishishan				
Zangbei Secondary		10,000+ per semester	1,411.8	Received money twice in the last two semesters. The second time: 30 yuan per student
Zangbei Primary		2,100	5,132	
Sanhe Teaching Point			1,310	The school was supposed to get 1,500 yuan per semester, but did not receive anything.
Hezheng				
Zhongmajia Teaching Point		509	2,545	School was supposed to get 1,700 + 250 yuan. Deduction was from 509 yuan for desk covers required by school district and for project supervision and review.
Kangle				
Sangjia Primary	2,328	3,370		Received extra 1,000 yuan for compensation of expenses for project supervision
Daojia Primary	3,748	2,800		
Majiazui Primary	1,475	1,475		
Gaolouzi Primary	2,128	1,590		It is reasonable for the district to deduct money, and it has happened before.

Despite this, school heads felt that their schools received less financial support from townships and villages. Before the tax reform, villages supported their schools with free water, electricity, etc., but after the reform the schools were themselves required to pay for everything. Changing political climates and macro-planning strategies could be seen to impact all the way down to the school level.

In summary, the Two Commitments are an important component of the GBEP, and seek in a far-sighted way to ensure long-term sustainability of various project components. The first commitment focuses on the total education budget, and the second focuses on non-personnel expenditures. Some officials have highlighted what they describe as difficulties with precise identification of what each commitment requires in each county, and implementation has been more straightforward in some counties than in others. However, the Two Commitments are clearly a major component of the project with political as well as technical significance.

The Scholarship Scheme

Compared with the Two Commitments, the scholarship scheme is more directly targeted at the needs of the poorest families, at girls, and at minorities. The following principles were established at the outset of the project.

- Girls should account for at least 70 per cent of scholarship recipients, and minority children should account for at least 60 per cent.
- In addition to poor children who are in school, the scheme aims to assist ones who are out of school either because they have dropped out or because they have never enrolled. In townships where the enrolment rate is below 60 percent, half of the scholarship funds must be used to support children who have never attended school.
- To be eligible, children must be from families with less than 300 yuan annual income and less than 300 grams of grain per capita. To select recipients, schools should use specific criteria weighted as follows: three points for girl, three points for

minority, two points for disabled parents, two points for single parent, three points for out of school, and four points for orphan. Girls would have the preference over boys when scores are equal.

- During the initial year (2000/01), in counties without universal primary education scholarships were to be used for primary school students only. Counties which were officially classified as having reached the threshold for universal primary education could use less than 20 per cent of the funds for junior middle schools, with all of these scholarships being awarded to girls.

- The maximum scholarship per semester was 50 yuan for primary school students and 75 yuan for secondary students. This was to be disbursed in kind, mainly in textbooks and stationery, rather than cash.

Scholarship funds were distributed to the four counties according to their income levels, the numbers of school-aged children in the population, and enrolment rates. Within the counties, funds were distributed according to a formula which had the following weights: poverty population 60 per cent, minority population 10 per cent, school enrolment (in absolute numbers) 15 per cent, and enrolment rate 15 per cent.

At the institutional level, schools were required to set up School Development Planning (SDP) committees for first-round selection of scholarship recipients. The responsibilities of the committees also included sensitising their communities. The committees submitted nominations to their school districts, which were supposed to check them and then submit them to the County PMOs for final approval. After the first year, the stipulation that girls should account for at least 70 per cent of scholarship reci-

Scholarships provided books and opportunities, especially to girls.

pients and that minority children should account for at least 60 per cent was replaced by a stipulation that all scholarships should be given to minority girls.

The scholarship scheme has had considerable visibility and some valuable successes. The positive case reported in Box 4 is one of many. A review conducted at the beginning of 2002 noted that the four counties had all made great strides in improving educational access, and that the scholarship scheme was a major component of this progress (Wang 2002b, p.7). One dimension about which the reviewer had been concerned was the possibility of negative social labelling of recipients. On this matter, however, she was reassured (Wang 2002b, pp.21-22):

> [In] general people take very positive attitude toward the program, and all of the interviewed recipients said that they'd never run into negative comments by other people including playmates and teachers because of the scholarship. In fact, on several occasions, the consultant was invited by community members to their houses, who argued that their children were in need of assistance too. It seems in general the program has no implications of negative social labeling in the project area.

This view was consistent with remarks made by most interviewees to the present authors. However, school heads did have the problem of convincing some households that they could not receive scholarships. "One father nagged me for a long time," reported one head. "I had to be persistent with all my powers of diplomacy, and to avoid taking criticism too personally."

It might be argued that one way for headteachers to protect themselves from criticisms in distribution of scholarships would be to use the committee structure prescribed by the regulations. The 2002 review of the scholarship scheme observed that, despite the specificity of the regulations which set out each step to be followed in admini-stration, the scheme lacked sufficient transparency and community involvement (Wang 2002b, p.7). The fact that regulations were not followed closely in all schools may have reflected on the one hand the demanding nature of the regulations and on the other hand the lack of such processes in the cultural traditions of the people concerned. Changes

---

Box 4: A Scholarship Gives a Chance in Life

Yang Meihua is in Grade 3 in one of the teaching points of Hezheng County. Her story started with sadness, and still has many challenges. However, at least it now has some hope. A major factor in this hope is the scholarship provided through the GBEP.

Four years ago, Meihua's father disappeared. He went to Tibet to earn some money as a labourer, and was never heard from again. This semester, all members of Meihua's class were asked to practise their literary skills by writing a letter. Meihua wrote to her father, even though she knew that she had nowhere to send the letter. "Why did you go, and never even communicate with us?", she asked. "Don't you know how much we need you? We guess you don't care about us any more...."

Without the father's income, life has been hard for the family. Meihua's mother has four mu of land, which is enough to feed the household. They need money to purchase medicines for Meihua's grandmother, so have had to borrow a sheep for breeding. Because they have no extra money for fertilisers, the land yields less than it might.

Under such circumstances, Meihua's family would never have been able to pay for her to go to school. Fortunately with the GBEP scholarship, schooling has now become possible. Meihua is the brightest in the class, and is much liked by her teachers.

Yet even with the scholarship, Meihua is in debt to the school. The fees are 70 yuan per semester, but the scholarship is only 50 yuan; and in addition, Meihua needs pencils and clothes that are not intolerably ragged. Meihua has not paid the debts to the school, and feels very anxious about them. Her mother admits that Meihua often cries at home.

Meihua will face further challenges soon. Her teaching point only goes up to Grade 4, so she would have to transfer to a primary school for Grade 5. The idea of then proceeding to secondary school may be an impossible dream. Yet she already has strong literacy skills and a wide understanding of the world. She has potential for a much brighter future than would have been the case if the GBEP scholarship had never come.

---

can be reinforced through workshops and other methods, but deep-seated cultural traditions of course cannot be overturned within a short period of time by a single project. An additional factor was that other scholarship schemes at the school level did not have the same requirements as the GBEP scholarship. This created some confusion.

The 2002 review added that the scholarship scheme had not adequately reached out-of-school children whose families were poor and deemed as having very low willingness and probability to enrol (Wang 2002b, p.7). Because of this, the report recommended review of the targeting strategy while at the same time stressing the need for realistic objectives. The report rightly noted (p.7) that "it might be too ambitious to expect that the program with limited amount of fund will be able to solve problems of educational opportunity for the most needy groups in the community".

Concerning the specific targets for the programme, the 2002 review noted that children in teaching points were generally poorer than their counterparts in village schools, that township centre schools were next on the scale, and that children in county schools were generally the least poor. The evaluation observed with satisfaction that the largest number of scholarships had been allocated to Dongxiang and Jishishan, and that in all four counties the largest share of scholarships was awarded to children in teaching points. However, it noted some problems. In line with the aspirations of the scheme, no scholarships had been awarded to children in county schools in Kangle, but in Jishishan 10.9 per cent of the children in county schools had received scholarships. Also, in Jishishan and Hezheng the largest numbers of scholarships as a proportion of enrolments went to children in town township centre schools. The evaluator had enquired about decision-making processes and was informed that in Dongxiang the county PMO, in the light of experience that district headteachers had tended to retain inappropriate shares of scholarships for their own schools, had centra-lised decisions and made their own allocations to the school level. In other counties, however, the PMOs had left decision-making to the district headteachers. The report noted that this might be the cause of the problematic distribution in Hezheng.

On the matter of gender, the evaluation did find that the principle that 70 per cent of scholarships should be allocated to girls had been followed (Table 13). However, the initial allocation proposed to the provincial PMO in December 2001 had not matched the objectives of the project, so the final list was the result of negotiation. Also, the evaluation noted that in one case the gender ratio aggregated at the district level did not match that on the application forms submitted by applicants via schools. The evaluation suggested that such twists and turns "indicate that to some extent there was perhaps a lack of self initiatives to implement, and a sense of ownership of, the policy to have girls as the priority of the assistance among teachers and PMO administrators". At least one head teacher considered the 70 per cent ratio of girls to be too high; and the evaluation also noted negative attitude toward education of girls not only among adults but also among primary school children.

Table 13: Distribution of Scholarships, by Gender, County and Level, 2001/02

		No. of scholarship recipients	No. of girl recipients	% girls
Primary	Jishishan	3,997	2,688	69.2
	Hezheng	1,544	1,087	70.4
	Kangle	2,076	1,537	74.0
	Dongxiang	4,184	3,135	74.9
	Total	*11,801*	*8,447*	*71.6*
Junior Middle	Jishishan	675	466	69.0
	Hezheng	763	703	92.1
	Kangle	1,209	869	71.9
	Dongxiang	583	419	71.9
	Total	*3,230*	*2,457*	*76.1*

Source: Wang (2002b), p.12.

Many of the points in the 2002 review matched the findings of the present authors during their school visits in 2003. However, during the intervening year the scheme had undergone some changes. Perhaps the most significant was adjustment in the scale of the scholarships in Dongxiang and Jishishan. Although the original regulations had stipulated that scholarships in all four counties could be up to a maximum of 50 yuan per primary school student per semester (i.e. 100 yuan per year), in practice the maximum had been taken as the standard. However, with the availability of subsidies to Dongxiang and Jishishan under the national government's compulsory education project, the scholarships for primary school students in those two counties were set at a maximum of 17.5 yuan per semester (i.e. 35 yuan per year).

The question whether these allocations were adequate will be addressed below. Meanwhile, it is noteworthy that the scholarships are in effect at a flat rate regardless of the depth of poverty. The authors encountered different views on the appropriateness of this policy. Some head teachers and other respondents suggested that it would be desirable to have different amounts to allow for the fact that some recipients were in greater need than others. "We need the discretion to give more help to the families which are desperately in need," argued one head teacher. However, other respondents felt that allocation of different amounts would increase the complexity of the scheme and open it to further possibilities of political manipulation. Our work is already difficult," reported another respondent, "and negotiations on the amount of the scholarships would make it more difficult still." Partly with the goal of satisfying a greater number of people, an additional response in at least one setting had been to take the total sum of the scholarships and then distribute subsidies to a larger number of recipients on a lower flat-rate basis, in contravention of the scholarship regulations.

Further complexities arise from the fact that, as noted, different scholarship schemes are in operation at the school level. In most schools the GBEP scholarships are the oldest scheme, but several schools also have scholarships from other sources. For example, in 2002/03:

- Beizhuangwan Primary School in Dongxiang County received 16 scholarships under the GBEP, 16 under the EU project, and 20 from the Mining Institute of Dalian. The EU scholarships were at the same rate as the GBEP ones; but the Dalian scholarships were 30 yuan per semester.
- Gongbeiwan Teaching Point in Dongxiang County received 21 GBEP scholarships at the rate of 17.5 yuan per semester, and 11 EU scholarships at 30 yuan.
- Sanhe Teaching Point in Jishishan County received 15 GBEP scholarships at the rate of 17.5 yuan per semester, 35 EU scholarships at 15 yuan, 13 scholarships from the Overseas Chinese Relief Project at 70 yuan, and one scholarship from the *Ai-De* foundation for 70 yuan.
- Mazhang Primary School in Hezheng County received 27 GBEP scholarships at the rate of 50 yuan per semester, and

another 13 scholarships from the national government's Compulsory Education Project at the same rate.

The potential for inequities in these instances was twofold. First was the problem of levels of payment: if one project came first and served the neediest, then the less needy pupils who were served later might actually receive higher amounts than the more needy.

The second problem was one of administration, namely that the payments to the schools had not always arrived according to the schedule. The cause of the problem lay at higher levels within the project administration, and the blockage was in due course cleared; but it caused difficulties for the target recipients of the scholarships. At the level of the specific schools listed above, the difficulty caused by the late payment included the fact that children who were presumably most in need (because they were in the first-initiated scholarship scheme) were not receiving payments while the other children did receive payments. Elsewhere, late payments caused difficulties for the administrators. One head teacher reported that:

> Some villagers have been suspicious about why they have not received the payments this semester. They suspected that either I or people further up the system have embezzled the money. This is really unfair on me, but there is nothing I can do.

The case of Beizhuangwan Primary School also helps to bring into focus the question whether the level of scholarship is adequate. The fees at this school were reported in Table 8, above. A GBEP scholarship of 17.5 yuan per semester was not enough to cover the fees of Grades 1 and 2, which were set at 25 yuan per semester; and the gap widened at Grades 3 to 5 for which the fees were 30 yuan. At the two schools in Jishishan, where the rate of GBEP scholarship was the same as in Dongxiang, the gap was even wider. The result is that some students have dropped out, while others have remained in the school but are in debt. In the case of the latter group, it is not uncommon for teachers themselves to pay the fees. The teachers have an incentive to do so, because otherwise enrolments drop and their own jobs could be at stake.

It does not seem reasonable for such a system to be institutionalised to the extent that teachers have to pay pupils' fees from their own meagre salaries.

In Hezheng and Kangle, the primary school scholarships were 50 yuan per semester, so the gap was smaller. Indeed in Gaolouzi Primary School the scholarship was greater than the fee, and in this school poor students were said to have been given pencils and other stationery from the scholarship money to make up the balance. Yet even in this school, which claimed that it could cover all direct costs, no effort was made to cover the opportunity costs of schooling.

Decisions on such matters are not simple, and it may be useful to look at experience elsewhere to gain insights. Various schemes have been tried in Pakistan, for example. In Balochistan Province, girls in primary schools have been given cooking oil as an incentive to attend school. In a scheme launched in 1996, girls were given five kilograms of oil per month if they had full attendance, and lower amounts if they had lower attendance. Funding constraints and administrative problems have given the scheme a chequered history, with phasing out in some districts, and suspension and restarts in others. Some participants are sceptical about the scheme, but others are more positive (Naz & Hussein 2003). In Sindh Province, a project launched in 1992 gave cash payments to girls in junior (Grades 6-8) and senior (Grades 9 and 10) secondary school. Again, however, the implementation proved problematic. The scholarships were perceived to be helpful in meeting the costs of schooling, but a significant proportion of the scholarships went to girls who were not the most in need. Also, evaluators remarked that the scholarship was not sufficient or predictable enough to serve as an incentive, given the lack of long-term financial or social gains expected from keeping girls in school (Ali et al. 1998, p.59).

Bangladesh is another country in which the authorities have given payments to children in order to encourage enrolments (World Bank 2000; Alam 2002; Kusakabe 2003). When launched in 1992, the scheme in Bangladesh provided food rather than cash. Each family with a child in school was given flour and rice, with a sliding scale according to the number of children in school. This food was given to the families rather than to the children, and thus is rather different from the GBEP's school lunch programme, which is discussed below. Knowing that adults rather than children are the decision-makers on whether children go to school, the scheme targeted the adults for receipt of the incentives. The scheme is credited with some success, though it also encountered difficulties. One difficulty was in administration, though perhaps a greater difficulty arose from politics when distributions became tied to the political affiliations of the recipients. In 1992 the scheme was re-placed with a cash distribution at a slightly lower rate than the value of the food that had previously been distributed. Even at this slightly lower rate, however, for most families the scheme did cover some opportunity costs as well as direct costs.

For the GBEP, the question whether the rate of scholarships should be raised to cover not only the full direct costs but also some of the opportunity costs merits detailed consideration. Such opportunity costs, following Wang's (2001) classification, might be in both Type 1 and Type 2 categories. In the process of consideration, one major factor for discussion should be sustainability of arrangements. In this respect, the functioning of the Two Commitments and wider issues of economic development and taxation become relevant. Another issue concerns the overall image of the government and the danger of excessive dependency. Bhutan is another country in which the government had provided food for school pupils but which decided in the mid-1990s to scale back its provision because it found households gaining excessive expec-tations of the government and becoming decreasingly self-reliant (Bray 1995); and related experiences have been noted in Lesotho (Sebatane & Caraher 2003). Nevertheless, a case can be made for at least short-term subsidies to selected families if appropriately targeted. As observed by the 2002 review of the scholarship programme (Wang 2002b, p.19):

> When children and their parents don't have enough food to eat, it might be indeed unrealistic to expect the parents to school their children; and the limited incentives of scholarship are not able to solve the most urgent needs of the families, which are stable and adequate sources of food.

This observation does, however, raise a further question about the ease of targeting. Experience in many settings has shown that the mechanics of targeting are rarely easy (see e.g. Besley & Kanbur 1990; Alderman et al. 1995; van de Walle 1998). One problem concerns the administrative and management costs of targeting, which may be excessive. Another problem is that the scale of opportunity costs may vary substantially from one family to another. Nevertheless, experience elsewhere shows that ways can be found to tackle such matters, and the GBEP has already in some respects addressed issues of targeting by steering scholarships away from county and township centre schools and towards village schools and teaching points. If higher scholarships were to be made available, one possibility might be to restrict them to children attending the teaching points on the grounds that these children are more likely to be in the poorest communities. Such an arrangement would undoubtedly exclude some poor children in other schools; but the search for a balance between administrative costs and the desire to reach the poorest households might still make it a desirable approach.

Boarding Allowances for Junior Middle School Girls

As a child goes up the education ladder, the cost of schooling increases. This is of course true of boys as well as girls; but the GBEP is particularly concerned about gender inequalities and the need to increase enrolment of girls. The project therefore includes a component which gives a boarding allowance to girls in junior middle schools.

The boarding allowance was launched in September 2002 on a pilot basis in one school in each of the four project counties. The allowance is for 75 yuan per student per semester (i.e. 150 yuan per year), and in the first year served 210 girls. The authors of this study visited Baizang Middle School in Jishishan to learn how it had implemented the scheme during its first year.

At the Baizang Middle School, the standard fees were 20 yuan for the general fee, 120 yuan for textbooks, and 50 yuan for use of computers. Boarders had to pay 50-60 yuan for food per month. A total of 114 girls, of whom 68 were of minority ethnicity, had been given boarding allowances. The criteria for selection had been a combination of distance and poverty.

Given that the boarding allowance scheme had been operating for only one year, and at the time of writing had only made one payment, it was too early to evaluate it. Nevertheless, the scheme seems an appropriate way to help to reduce the burden on some poor households. As with the scholarship scheme, however, the boarding allowance does not cover the full direct costs of boarding, let alone the indirect costs. The same issues of sustainability arise as with the scholarship scheme; but implementation of the Two Commitments could be a way to resolve these issues.

The Textbook Revolving Fund

Recognising that textbooks impose a heavy burden on many families, the Textbook Revolving Fund (TRF) aims to help low-income families to secure books at reduced cost. The scheme was launched following a workshop in April 2000. Workshop participants had some hesitation about the scheme, noting that:

- The standard textbooks have low quality paper and bindings, and are easily damaged. It is thus difficult to reuse them.
- Textbooks are designed to be used as exercise books as well as texts, with students using pages for working out problems and practising skills.
- The contents of textbooks are being constantly revised, and old books may therefore not fit the curriculum requirements each year.
- Students commonly use simple schoolbags in which books are put together with potatoes, fried dough and water bottles. This contributes to the short life of textbooks.
- There was a danger that students would use the books less frequently in order to protect books for the TRF, which would then impact on learning quality.
- Considerable management costs would be incurred by the collection and storage of textbooks.
- Used books are less appealing, and may make their owners feel disadvantaged.

- Students in Grades 3 to 5 may wish to retain their textbooks in order to prepare for the primary school graduation examinations.

Despite the misgivings reflected in this list, a later workshop in 2000 was more enthusiastic. According to the report on the workshop, parents of all backgrounds who participated in the discussions "overwhelmingly welcomed the idea of TRF". With this encouragement, the project authorities decided to launch the scheme on a pilot basis in Baihe District of Dongxiang, Xiaoguan District of Jishishan, Taizijie Primary School of Hezheng, and Kangfeng District of Kangle. The GBEP provided a sum of money for organisers of the TRF to purchase the textbooks used by students in the preceding year, with the idea that the books would then be sold at prices lower than those of new books. The procedures for identifying students to benefit from the TRF were designed to be similar to those for identifying students for scholarships, i.e. priority in the purchase of the second-hand books was to be given to low-income children and particularly girls from minority ethnic groups.

However, evaluation in 2002 showed that many of the original misgivings had indeed been justified. In Dongxiang, although a survey two years previously had suggested that 500 to 600 students would like to use second-hand books, few actually did purchase the books. The headteacher of the pilot school had collected 206 sets of Chinese and mathematics books covering all grades from nine schools in the district, but only 35 sets were procured by students and 13 of these had not been paid for. In Hezheng 118 sets of books from Grades 3 and 4 were collected for all subjects, but only 39 sets had been sold to students. Four of those students were in fact "assigned" the books because their school had underestimated the numbers to be ordered from the bookstore, and those students were not given discounted prices. Daojia Primary School in Kangle collected 91 sets of books, but was only able to sell five of them.

Xiaoguan School District in Jishishan had a more positive view. Much effort was put into purchasing 400 books from primary schools in rich areas outside the district in order to pump-prime the experiment. The collected books were then delivered to poor students within the school district for free. Over a period of five semesters, 537 students were said to have benefited. In financial terms, the cost of the operation was very modest at 300 yuan. However, the pilot consumed a great deal of time and energy.

A further complication noted by the 2002 Mid-Term Review (GBEP 2002, section 2.3) was that the state provided textbooks free of charge to pupils in Dongxiang and Jishishan because those counties were deemed not to have reached the official threshold for universal primary education. Observing that the TRF had encountered many difficulties despite some successes, the Mid-Term Review concluded that it would be necessary to consider how to readjust the scheme.

The observations of the present authors echo those of the earlier evaluators and of the Mid-Term Review. The team visited three schools which had been part of the pilot, and also spoke about the matter to teachers and pupils in non-pilot schools. The findings were not encouraging. In addition to the list of challenges presented at the April 2000 workshop is a cultural issue. The authors were informed that Muslim students were unwilling to use second-hand books because they feared that the books might have been used by Han and other non-Muslim students who could have been handling pork and not washed their hands thoroughly.

The authors noted that in addition to the problems of running the scheme at the school level were problems with the mechanism for securing books from the sole supplier, Xinhua. This supplier has outlets throughout the country, and in Gansu has a monopoly. Through large-scale production Xinhua is able to produce books at low cost, and its pricing structure may benefit remote schools which would otherwise have to pay much higher transportation costs than their less remote counterparts. However, Xinhua is only willing to sell books in sets, and requires advance orders for doing so. The situation is thus very different from situations in which individual books are readily available through multiple outlets in the market place.

That Xinhua does have some flexibility is evident from an AusAid-UNICEF scheme which operates in Kangle and one other (non-GBEP) county in the province, and which also has some lessons for the GBEP. The AusAid-UNICEF scheme arranged for printing of the standard textbooks in Chinese and Arithmetic, but with better quality paper and production. The books are certainly more attractive than the standard issue, and the idea was that each book would be part of a revolving scheme with a life span sufficient to serve three cohorts of students. These books in fact only revolved once, thereby serving two cohorts. The county Bureau of Education was able to make an arrangement with Xinhua for Chinese and Arithmetic to be excluded from the sets of books sold to the schools and students, and the AusAid-UNICEF books were provided free of charge. However, the AusAid-UNICEF scheme in some respects suffered the same fate as the GBEP scheme, even though the AusAid-UNICEF books were more durable. The biggest problems were first that the syllabus changed, and second that the textbooks were also designed to be used as workbooks. Children had been asked to do the workbook parts in separate exercise books, but many did not follow that instruction, with the result that pupils who received the textbooks in their second time of usage found that the arithmetic problems had already been worked out by their predecessors and that the "fill in the blanks" parts of the Chinese books had already been filled in.

The Free-Lunch Programme

The free-lunch programme was launched in 2002 as a pilot in Duanling Teaching Point and Beizhuangwan Primary School in Dongxiang County, and in Gahejia and Sanhe Teaching Points in Jishishan County. At the time of the visit to Gansu by the authors of this study it had been operating for one academic year. During the month in which the programme was launched, a baseline survey was conducted (Wang & Dang 2002). The pro-

Free lunch

gramme reduces costs to households by reducing the amount of food which the households would otherwise have to provide. The programme also aims to improve the diet of the pupils, and to reduce the distraction to their learning that would be caused by hunger. Some benefits already realised in some schools are a shorter school day and less travelling as children do not need to return home at lunchtime.

When the scheme was launched, at Gahejia and Sanhe Teaching Points the lunch consisted of one egg and one mantou (bun) per student. However, the students in Sanhe did not like the mantou, in part because the hygiene of the cook was felt to be poor. The lunch was then changed to one egg and one bag of quick noodles. This remained the standard for another few months, but was again changed because quick noodles have a low nutrition value. The lunch at the time of the authors' visit was one egg and one cake.

The cost of each lunch is just under one yuan per pupil per day. Thus over a whole academic year the cost would be approximately 200 yuan per pupil (i.e. over five times the amount of each primary school scholarship in these two counties). However, in practice this does not relieve of a burden of 150 yuan from the recipients' household budgets, because in the absence of the free lunch the children would eat lower-cost items.

At the time of writing, the free-lunch programme had only operated on a pilot basis in four schools and had not yet been comprehensively reviewed. From the perspective of the financial burden on poor households, the programme does have some merits. However, a review would again have to consider the matter of targeting. One of the four institutions in which the programme is piloted is on a tarred road and serves a community which is certainly not among the poorest of the poor. As currently organised, the free-lunch scheme was institutional in basis, and therefore covered the not-so-poor children in those institutions as well as the poor. If it remains institutional, it might be better to focus only on the institutions which can be demonstrated to serve the poorest communities.

Alternatively, the financial resources devoted to the free-lunch programme could instead by converted to scholarships which can target poor families more precisely. The head of one village served by one of the pilot schools is worth recording. "The free lunch gets people's attention," he reported, "but it would be better to give them free tuition." This perspective dovetailed with that of an administrator in a county PMO:

> The danger of the programme is that villagers feel that even food is provided free of charge by the government. If resources are scarce, perhaps the money should be put into free textbooks so that the children can learn from those books.

However, on the other side of the balance sheet are the nutritional and learning benefits from giving food to hungry children. Also, when all children are fed, those who are from poor families are not made to feel conspicuous.

Energy-Saving Buildings

The standard classroom designs in GBEP projects have large south-facing windows in order to maximise heat gain during winter, and improved insulation in order to minimise heat loss. The design is relevant to this study insofar as it reduces the need for heating by coal or other needs. Where heating is required, in many schools the pupils are charged for the cost of fuel in their school fees. In other schools, pupils are asked to bring bricks of coal from their homes. In both cases the arrangement imposes a cost on the pupils' households.

A GBEP evaluation in the four counties in December 2002 sought to compare the temperatures in the project classrooms with those in comparable classrooms with other designs. Research assistants were asked to place one thermometer on the south side of the front blackboard and another thermometer at the same side of the rear blackboard. They were also asked to place a thermometer outside, at the back of the classroom in the shade, and to place coal stoves in the middle of the classroom. Temperatures were then recorded each day at 10.00 am and at 3.00 pm, and matched with the coal

The pilot solar-energy building

consumption each day.

It was difficult to carry out the evaluation with complete consistency, in part because few schools had both old and new classrooms with otherwise identical characteristics. Also, coal-burning stoves are not precise instruments, and the amount of heat that they generate varies according to the inclinations and skills of the operators. Nevertheless, the evaluation did show that the GBEP classrooms were on average approximately 2 degrees Celsius warmer than the other classrooms.

In addition to the standard classrooms is one particular design, used in Gaolouzi Primary School, Kangle County. Two buildings in this school, which were constructed in September 2001, use solar panels to heat the classrooms. Each classroom has a floor area of 234 square metres.

An evaluation of the effectiveness of the experimental passive solar classrooms was conducted in 2002 by Gao Fang of the Gansu Global Energy Saving & Developing Technique Institute (Gao 2002). The study noted that the cost per square metre of the classrooms was 718.00 yuan, of which 485.50 yuan was for civil works, 15.95 yuan was for electrical lighting, and 216.60 yuan was for the solar heating systems. The solar heating systems thus comprised 30.2 per cent of the total cost. Construction of normal classrooms at the location would have cost 550 to 600 yuan per square metre. Thus, the experimental classrooms cost 25 per cent more to construct than ordinary classrooms. However, the classrooms were considerably warmer. In winter the average temperature at 10.00 am was 6.8 degrees Celsius inside, compared with -6.6 degrees outside; and at 4.00 pm respective temperatures were 7.9 degrees and -1.5 degrees. As a result, the school did not need to charge households so much for heating classrooms.

While these results from the solar classrooms are impressive, they have to be set against the extra cost of the classrooms. Gao did indicate some ways in which the cost could be reduced, including through the use of locally-produced insulating materials and replacement of fire-burned bricks by adobe blocks. Nevertheless, even with these cost-reductions the extra cost of the solar classrooms may be too high to justify widespread usage.

Also worth noting is that despite the goal of the project to focus particularly on minorities and on low-enrolment communities, the school selected for the experimental solar classroom was chosen partly on the grounds of accessibility rather than other factors. The school entirely populated by Han pupils and teachers, and claims a 100 per cent enrolment and graduation rate. This figure is commendable, and the school adds that the enrolment rate has been raised from 97 per cent before the project. However, the extra costs of this particular experimental classroom were not targeted to alleviate the burden on poor minority children.

Other Components

The other project components are not directly related to strategies to alleviate the financial burden on households, but some do deserve remark as having some relation to aspects of economics. Chief among them are the components which improve the quality of education. These are relevant because they are a major determinant of whether the schooling is worth receiving. The authorities press all families to send their children to school, and the poorest households which respond to these exhortations make great financial and other sacrifices. Circumstances would indeed be tragic if those sacrifices were to be in vain because the quality of education was so poor. Thus, the project components which raise the quality of education through teacher training and other approaches are also of considerable relevance to the economic equation for poor households. They cannot be quantified in this study, but at least their existence must be noted.

The capital works programme can also help reduce burdens on households. Before the GBEP, children at Baizang Primary School were required to bring their own desks to school, but now the project provides sturdy desks for all children.

Also deserving specific mention are components which seek to enhance community involvement. China has been through various cycles in the balance between government and community inputs to schooling. As the role of the state has increased, there has been a tendency for the roles of communities correspondingly to decrease (Robinson 1988; Hannum 2003). In some schools that the authors visited during the preparation of this study, links between schools and communities appeared to be minimal.

In other schools, however, links were clearly more vigorous, and had been promoted in particular by the School Development Planning (SDP) components of the project. Head teachers and their staffs had been actively encouraged to solicit inputs from communities, and those inputs had played a

School Development Planning Groupwork

role in resourcing as well as other domains. For example, the community of Majiazai Primary School in Kangle County has invested the equivalent of 25,000 yuan in a sturdy 170-metre wall and gate, has flattened the ground, and had installed 200 metres of water pipes. Community inputs are not always pro-poor, and in some settings community involvement widens rather than narrows gaps (Bray 1996b, 2003). However, if well managed community inputs can be harnessed to help low-income households. The head teacher of Majiazai Primary School indicated that the community serving his school had strong potential in this domain. Similarly, the Party Secretary in one village serving Beizhuangwan Primary School declared: "People in this community would be pleased to assist the school with resourcing, but they have never been asked."

More generally, the potential from community involvement was highlighted by a team from Northwest Normal University (2002, p.57) who had been commissioned to evaluate progress in the GBEP:

> The villagers said that it is the first time in the history of the community that the community people are consulted on a systematic basis on the issue of the school development. The community members have changed their it-has-nothing-to-do-with-me attitudes to active participation. The members in the community feel that they are the masters of their own school and

they should make their own contributions to the development of the school.

The review added that in Chuntaibeizhuang and Gongbeiwan of Dongxiang County, the communities had provided girl students with free textbooks; and the cadres and religious leaders in Bayanggou had offered assistance to two students from poor families. Of course this has not worked uniformly, and much depends on personalities as well as structures. However, it is an indication of further potential for the future.

Conclusions

This study has focused on the financial burden that schooling imposes on household budgets, and it is particularly concerned with the burden on poor households. The financial burden is a major reason why some children in the four counties have never attended school and why other children have either dropped out or are in danger of doing so. This pattern resembles that in many other underdeveloped parts of the world.

The financial burden is of course not the only reason for non-attendance. Indeed, as remarked by several interviewees, it may not even be the most important. Other factors include general traditions and perceptions on the usefulness or otherwise of schooling. To address this, one village head interviewed by the team indicated the value of setting a demonstration effect by persuading key families to send their children to school. However, concerning the economic justifications for sending children to school, that village head was ambivalent. "We can argue that schooling equips young people to go out for paid employment", he remarked, "but then they will have to leave the village, and this can create social problems." Moreover, specifically on the matter of girls' education he lamented the lack of local positive examples:

> In this village, two girls have graduated from primary school. They looked for jobs as workers, but they were not successful. We thus do not have a demonstration effect in this village of the economic benefits from educating girls.

The economic benefits can of course reach beyond paid employment, and many people would argue that the investment in schooling can assist with self-employed trade and agriculture. However, the evidence is not always convincing at the household level; and even if poor householders were to be convinced, they might still consider the potential benefits to be beyond their reach. The poorest of the poor simply do not have the resources to commit to long-term investments when pressed by the demands of basic daily survival.

In such circumstances, the focus must return to the basic rationales for the advocacy of universal education. From the perspective of the State, the rationales are at least partially based on a desire for citizens' participation in the cash economy and civic society, and for avoidance of the instability that could result from excessive social inequalities. This being the case, it is arguable that the State should be the main provider of the resources for education. The difficulty in China is that the State finds itself resource-constrained in the face of multiple competing priorities.

The GBEP has helped to bridge this gap. It has also had a significant impact not only in providing capital works and other elements of infrastructure but also in experimentation to try new approaches. Some experiments have been more successful than others; but even the less successful ones have had the benefit of stimulating innovative thinking.

In the domain of financing, the Two Commitments are a major component which deserve attention not only by the administrators of the GBEP in its remaining years but also by other projects both in China and elsewhere. Implementation of the Two Commitments has not proven to be a straightforward matter, and this component of the GBEP cannot yet be described as an unqualified success. Some funds are flowing to the school level because of the Two Commitments, and this component has potential to ensure that government resources do take up the slack from the GBEP as the external resources phase out. However, a great deal depends on the overall financial health of the counties, on political decision-making at various levels, and on the implementation capacity of the administrative machinery. Continued focus on these matters will be needed during the remaining life of the GBEP, and other projects which seek to imitate the GBEP should not underestimate the complexities involved.

At the school level, the scholarship component is perhaps a more visible and easily-comprehended instrument for reaching the poorest households. From a systems perspective, it is instructive to note how a single central idea in a project document can turn into a kaleidoscope of variations at the school level which changes over time in response to differing conditions in different localities. The scholarship programme deserves to be maintained as a mechanism through which the State alleviates the burden on the poorest, and also provides incentives to not-so-poor minorities and to households with girls to send their children to school.

This study has nevertheless suggested that the scholarship programme can be refined to improve its targeting. It has also raised the question whether the value of the scholarships should be increased to enable them to cover all of the direct costs and perhaps also some or all of the opportunity costs of schooling. Again, it is arguable that since universalisation of education chiefly serves the goals of the State, then the State should pay for this. The experience of other countries suggests that in due course the State would be able to phase out payment of opportunity costs for at least the majority of recipients, since only the poorest of the poor would find these opportunity costs prohibitive (as opposed to merely discouraging) of schooling at the primary level.

At the secondary level, however, the challenges are larger and are likely to persist for considerably longer. Although the GBEP focuses on the full period of basic education, including junior middle schooling, the present study has concentrated on the primary level since that is the initial step deserving priority attention. When further achievements have been accomplished at the primary level, it will become necessary in due course to shift the balance of attention towards junior middle schooling.

Meanwhile, other components of the project which have been given attention in this study include the textbook revolving fund and the free-lunch programme. These components are less effective in reducing the burden on poor households. Efforts have not been wasted, especially since reduction of the financial burden is only one objective of the components, and useful lessons have been learned from experience.

However, the two schemes are demanding not only in financial terms but also in management at all levels of the system.

In closing, the authors applaud the architects and the implementers of the GBEP for their great achievements during the life of the project. Some parts have of course worked better than others; but the overall impact of the project is clear for all to see. The lessons are useful not only to similar projects in Gansu but also to projects in other parts of China and elsewhere.

Appendix:
School Development Planning in the GBEP

Aims

School Development Planning (SDP) aims to bring schools and local communities together to create a unified approach to school development. The SDP in particular aims to change the relationship between the school and the county (the funding tier of local government) from a traditionally 'top down' one to a more 'bottom-up' one. It does this by giving schools more involvement in their own development. It also aims to change the relationship between schools and communities by bringing them closer together and focusing on some of the social development aspects of education that prevent children entering, staying and achieving in schools.

Training

Training materials for trainers and trainees have been prepared by consultants working closely with Project Management Office (PMO) staff. These included trainers' manual, an SDP guidelines booklet, and a format for schools to complete their school development plans. Head teachers and School District Directors have been trained in new skills to help bring schools and communities together and identify common issues. These skills included:

- Participatory Approaches (PA) involving all members of school and community and especially those traditionally marginalised in planning,
- generic training skills and practical knowledge, and
- training in three key PA tools for work with communities, namely (i) *social maps*, which are a simple way of visualising issues of access; (ii) *problem trees*, which help to link problems, causes and effects in a clear and logical way; and (iii) *ranking*, to make sure all voices and opinions have a fair hearing.

Financing

In the first three years of the project, DFID funding provided some hardware and software to schools. Gradually this funding has been replaced by the counties themselves through the Two Commitments.

In 2002, schools started to receive some funding based on a pupil-weighted formula which emphasised the needs of poorer schools first. The size of the funding delegated was designed gradually to increase over the remainder of the project.

Summary and Comment

Initial responses to SDP were very positive. During the first three years, three rounds of SDP were completed with all 671 schools having produced plans at least twice.

SDP has the potential to transform the delivery of rural education in ways which have far reaching impacts on the social, economic and cultural life of the communities schools serve. By changing the traditional nature of the relationships between schools and their communities, and between schools and the education administration, SDP provides an effective vehicle for the modernisation of rural education.

Traditionally, the education administration system has been centralised and schools have had almost no say in internal management. Even though the current system is apparently decentralised, schools have to pay close attention to requests from county education bureaux. At same time, links between the schools and the communities they are supposed to serve are weak, in part because the communities treat the schools as organisations belonging to the upper-level governments.

The mechanism developed in the GBEP tries to break down the barriers between schools and their communities and to strengthen the autonomy of schools. This is something new in China and the pilot in the four project counties showed very positive effects. The greatest success with the pilot was the use of participatory approaches in doing SDP, which gave local people – and particularly groups normally disadvantaged and disregarded – a chance to have a say on school affairs for the first time in decades. Some local resources were also mobilised to support school development. The closer linkage between school and community in the counties contributed significantly to the increased enrolment rate, reduced drop-out rate, and much stronger sense of the value of education to parents.

The relationship between the schools and local education authorities also changed as the schools gained autonomy and began to decide how to make best use the limited resources from the government allocations, especially the funds from the non-personnel funds. This helped to reduce the parents' burden in paying the miscellaneous fees for school operation.

The final goal of this innovative practice is to change the traditional ideology from one of serving the education bureaux to one of serving the people. In this way, the development of schools can be combined with community development. There are many challenges ahead, but the greatest is to change the administration style of local education authorities from giving orders to providing service to schools.

References

Alam, Mahbubul A.K.M. (2002): 'Stipend Programme: Its Overall Impact in Primary Education Sector in Bangladesh'. Dhaka: Bangladesh Public Administration Training Centre.

Alderman, H., Behrman, J.R., Khan, S., Ross, D.R. & Sabot, R. (1995): 'Public Schooling Expenditures in Rural Pakistan: Efficiently Targeting Girls and a Lagging Region', in van de Walle, Dominique & Nead, Kimberly (eds.), *Public Spending and the Poor: Theory and Evidence*. Baltimore: The Johns Hopkins University Press, pp.187-221.

Ali, M., Farah, I., Ostberg, S., Penny, A. & Smith, R. (1998): 'Some Lessons from Experience: A Report of a Joint Research Programme for the Norwegian Agency for Development Cooperation'. Karachi: Institute for Educational Development, Aga Khan University.

Asian Development Bank (2001): *Education and National Development: Trends, Issues, Policies, and Strategies*. Manila: Asian Development Bank.

Besley, Timothy & Kanbur, Ravi (1990): *The Principles of Targeting*. WPS 385, Washington DC: The World Bank.

Boyle, S., Brock, A., Mace, J. & Sibbons, M. (2002): *Reaching the Poor: The 'Costs' of Sending Children to School – A Six Country Comparative Study*. Educational Papers No.47, London: Department for International Development.

Bray, Mark (1995): *The Costs and Financing of Primary Schooling in Bhutan*. Thimphu: Ministry of Health & Education and UNICEF.

Bray, Mark (1996a): *Counting the Full Cost: Parental and Community Financing of Education in East Asia*. Washington DC: The World Bank in collaboration with UNICEF [Chinese translation by Hu Wenbin published 2000 by Beijing Normal University Press].

Bray, Mark (1996b): *Decentralization of Education: Community Financing*. Washington DC: The World Bank.

Bray, Mark (2002): *The Costs and Financing of Education: Trends and Policy Implications*. Series 'Education in Developing Asia'. Manila: Asian Development Bank, and Hong Kong: Comparative Education Research Centre, The University of Hong Kong.

Bray, Mark (2003): 'Government and Household Financing of Education: Finding Appropriate Balances', in Min Weifang, Yang Zhoufu & Li Wenli (eds.), *Raising Adequate Resources for Education*. Beijing: People's Education

Press, pp.605-631 [Chinese translation by Li Mei in *Peking University Education Review*, Vol.1, No.2, pp.43-51].

Bruns, B., Mingat, A. & Rakotomalala, R. (2003): *Achieving Universal Primary Education by 2015: A Chance for Every Child*. Washington DC: The World Bank.

China, People's Republic of (1985): *Reform of China's Educational Structure: Decision of the CPC Central Committee*. Beijing: Foreign Languages Press.

China, People's Republic of (1986): *Law of the People's Republic of China on Compulsory Education*. Beijing: State Education Commission.

China, People's Republic of (2000): *National Report for EFA 2000 Assessment*. Beijing: Ministry of Education and National Commission for UNESCO.

Colclough, C., Rose, P. & Tembon, M. (2000): 'Gender Inequalities in Primary Schooling: The Roles of Poverty and Adverse Cultural Practice'. *International Journal of Educational Development*, Vol.20, No.1, pp.5-27.

Croll, Elisabeth J. (2001): 'Amartya Sen's 100 Million Missing Women'. *Oxford Development Studies*, Vol.29, No.3, pp.225-244.

Deininger, Klaus (2003): 'Does Cost of Schooling Affect Enrollment by the Poor? Universal Primary Education in Uganda'. *Economics of Education Review*, Vol.22, No.3, pp.291-305.

DFID [Department for International Development] (2001): *The Challenge of Universal Primary Education: Strategies for Achieving the International Development Targets*. London: Department for International Development.

Gansu Basic Education Project (GBEP) (2002): 'Mid-Term Review on the Progress of the Gansu Basic Education Project (GBEP): Synthesis Report'. Lanzhou: Gansu Basic Education Project.

Gao Fang (2002): 'UK/China Gansu Basic Education Project: Study Report of Passive Solar Classrooms Cost Reduction'. Lanzhou: Gansu Global Energy Saving & Developing Technique Institute.

Gertler, Paul & Glewwe, Paul (1991): 'The Willingness to Pay for Education for Daughters in Contrast to Sons: Evidence from Rural Peru'. *The World Bank Economic Review*, Vol.6, No.1, pp.171-188.

Gladney, Dru (1999): 'Making Muslims in China: Education, Islamicization and Representation, in Postiglione, Gerard A. (ed.) *China's National Minority Education: Culture, Schooling, and Development*. New York: Falmer Press, pp.55-94.

Han Shutian (1990): 'Primary School Education', in *Education in Contemporary China*. Changsha: Hunan Education Publishing House, pp.190-258.

Hannum, Emily (2003): 'Poverty and Basic Education in Rural China: Villages, Households, and Girls' and Boys' Enrollment'. *Comparative Education Review*, Vol.47, No.2, pp.141-159.

Hyde, Karin A.L. (2001): *Girls' Education*. Thematic Study for the World Education Forum, Dakar, Senegal. Paris: UNESCO.

Kusakabe, Tatsuya (2003): 'The Acceptance of Primary Education in Bangladesh: Focus on Conflict with Islamic Madrasa Schools'. *Comparative Education Research*, Vol.29, pp.169-185. [in Japanese]

Law Wing Wah (2000): 'Schooling and Social Change: The People's Republic of China', in Mazurek, K., Winzer, M. & Majorek, C. (eds.), *Education in a Global Society: A Comparative Perspective*. Boston: Allyn & Bacon, pp.355-370.

Lee, W.O. (2002): *Equity and Access to Education: Themes, Tensions, and Policies*. Series 'Education in Developing Asia'. Manila: Asian Development Bank, and Hong Kong: Comparative Education Research Centre, The University of Hong Kong.

Liu Fengshu (2004): 'Basic Education in China's Rural Areas: A Legal Obligation or an Individual Choice?'. *International Journal of Educational Development*, Vol.24, No.1, pp.5-21.

Ma Wanhua & Zheng Zhenzhen (2003): 'Why do they Stop Schooling? A Case Study of Girls' Dropout in a County of Hebei Province'. *Peking University Education Review*, Vol.1, No.3, pp.70-76. [in Chinese]

Mehrotra, Santosh & Delamonica, Enrique (1998): 'Household Costs and Public Expenditure on Primary Education in Five Low Income Countries: A Comparative Analysis'. *International Journal of Educational Development*, Vol.18, No.1, pp.41-61.

Naz, Samina & Hussein, Ashfaq (2003): information given to Mark Bray, Institute for Educational Development, Aga Khan University, Karachi, 29 August.

Northwest Normal University, Case Study Group (2002): 'Cross-Case Analysis Report'. Lanzhou: Gansu Basic Education Project.

Penrose, Perran (1998): *Cost Sharing in Education: Public Finance, School and Household Perspectives*. Educational Papers No.27, London: Department for International Development.

Postiglione, Gerard A. (1999): 'Introduction: State Schooling and Ethnicity in China', in Postiglione, Gerard A. (ed.) *China's National Minority Education: Culture, Schooling, and Development.* New York: Falmer Press, pp.3-19.

Robinson, Jean C. (1988): 'State Control and Local Financing of Schools in China', in Bray, Mark with Lillis, Kevin (eds.), *Community Financing of Education: Issues and Policy Implications in Less Developed Countries.* Oxford: Pergamon Press, pp.181-195.

Sebatane, E. Molapi & Caraher, Martin (2003): 'Complexities of Evaluating Overlapping Social Service Programmes: The Case of School Feeding Schemes in Lesotho Primary Schools', paper presented at the Oxford International Conference on Education and Development, 9-11 September.

Tsang, Mun C. (1997): 'Cost Analysis for Improved Policymaking and Evaluation'. *Educational Evaluation and Policy Analysis*, Vol.19, No.4, pp.318-324.

Tsang, Mun C. & Ding Yanqing (2003): 'Financial Challenges in Compulsory Education and Intergovernmental Education Grants'. *Peking University Education Review*, Vol.1, No.1, pp.84-94. [in Chinese]

UNESCO (2000): *A Synthesis Report of Education for All 2000 Assessment in the East and South East Asia Sub-Region.* Bangkok: UNESCO Principal Regional Office for Asia and the Pacific.

UNESCO (2001): *World Education Forum, Dakar, Senegal 26-28 April 2000: Final Report.* Paris: UNESCO.

UNESCO (2002): *Education for All: Is the World on Track?* Paris: UNESCO.

UNESCO (2003): *Gender and Education for All: The Leap to Equality.* EFA Global Monitoring Report 2003/4. Paris: UNESCO.

van de Walle, Dominique (1998): 'Targeting Revisited'. *The World Bank Research Observer*, Vol.13, No.2, pp.237-248.

Wang Juan & Dang Dengfeng (2002): 'Gansu Basic Education Project (GBEP): Free School Lunch Pilot Baseline Study Report'. Lanzhou: College of Education Science, Northwest Normal University.

Wang Rong (2002a): 'Political Dimensions of County Government Budgeting in China: A Case Study'. paper presented at the Social Policy Development conference, 25-26 March, Institute of Development Studies, University of Sussex, Brighton, UK.

Wang Rong (2002b): 'GBEP Scholarship Program Review Report'. Lanzhou: Gansu Basic Education Project.

Wang Rong, Yue Changjun & Li Wenli (2003): 'China's Educational Finance System: Challenges and Reforms'. *Peking University Education Review*, Vol.1, No.2, pp.73-80 (Part 1); Vol.1, No.3, pp.77-82 (Part 2). [in Chinese]

Wang Shanmai (2001): 'Cost Sharing Study: Gansu Basic Education Project (GBEP)'. Beijing: Center for Education & Economy Research, Beijing Normal University.

Williams, Peter (1983): 'The Last Ten Per Cent'. *International Review of Education*, special issue on 'The Universalization of Primary Education', Vol. 29, No.2, pp.159-163.

World Bank, The (2000): *Bangladesh Education Sector Review*. Dhaka: The World Bank/University Press Ltd.

World Bank, The (2001): 'China: Provincial Expenditure Review'. Washington DC: The World Bank.

Zhou Daming, Mei Fangquan & Huang Ping (2003): 'Social Assessment Report of China Proposed Basic Education in Western Areas Project for Preparation of Ethnic Minority Education Strategy'. Report to DFID and the World Bank, Beijing.

Notes on the Authors

Mark BRAY is Dean of the Faculty of Education at the University of Hong Kong. Among his specialisms is the economics and financing of basic education. He has conducted consultancy assignments in over 50 countries for the Asian Development Bank (ADB), British Council, Commonwealth Secretariat, Department for International Development (DFID), UNESCO, UNICEF, World Bank and other bodies. He has also published extensively in the fields of educational planning and comparative education. Address: Faculty of Education, The University of Hong Kong, Pokfulam Road, Hong Kong. E-mail: mbray@hku.hk.

DING Xiaohao is Head of the Economics of Education Department in the Faculty of Education of Peking University. She holds several awards for excellence in research, and has published extensively in the domains of economics and financing of education. She has been a consultant on several World Bank projects, and also has strong international experience. Address: Faculty of Education, Peking University, Beijing 100871. E-mail: xiaohao.ding@263.net.

HUANG Ping is Deputy Director of the Institute of Sociology of the Chinese Academy of Social Sciences. He is widely known and highly respected both in China and internationally for his work in social development, which has particularly focused on education, health, community development and migration. He has conducted many consultancy assignments in China and in other parts of the Asian region for the ADB, DFID, FAO, UNESCO, and World Bank, and for non-governmental organisations such as World Vision. He has also published extensively, and is Chief Executive Editor of the monthly periodical *Reading*. Address: Institute of Sociology, Chinese Academy of Social Sciences, 5 Jianguomen Nei Dajie, Beijing 100732. E-mail: huangping @cass.org.cn.

CERC Publications

Series: CERC Monographs

1. Yoko Yamato (2003): *Education in the Market Place: Hong Kong's International Schools and their Mode of Operation.* ISBN 962-8093-57-6. 117pp. HK$100 / US$16.
2. Mark Bray, Ding Xiaohao & Huang Ping (2004): *Reducing the Burden on the Poor: Household Costs of Basic Education in Gansu, China.* ISBN 962-8093-32-0. 67pp. HK$50 / US$10. (Also available in Chinese)
3. Maria Manzon (2004): *Building Alliances: Schools, Parents and Communities in Hong Kong and Singapore.* ISBN 962-8093-36-3. HK$100 / US$16.
4. Mark Bray & Seng Bunly (2005): *Balancing the Books: Household Financing of Basic Education in Cambodia.* ISBN 962-8093-39-8. HK$100 / US$16.

Series: Education in Developing Asia

1. Don Adams (2002): *Education and National Development: Priorities, Policies, and Planning.* ISBN 971-561-403-5. 81pp. HK$100 / US$12 each or HK$400 / US$50 for set of five.

2. David Chapman (2002): *Management and Efficiency in Education: Goals and Strategies.* ISBN 971-561-404-3. 60pp. HK$100 / US$12 each or HK$400 / US$50 for set of five.

3. Mark Bray (2002): *The Costs and Financing of Education: Trends and Policy Implications.* ISBN 971-561-405-1. 77pp. HK$100 / US$12 each or HK$400 / US$50 for set of five.

4. W.O. Lee (2002): *Equity and Access to Education: Themes, Tensions, and Policies.* ISBN 971-561-406-X. 101pp. HK$100 / US$12 each or HK$400 / US$50 for set of five.

5. David Chapman & Don Adams (2002): *The Quality of Education: Dimensions and Strategies.* ISBN 971-561-407-8. 72pp. HK$100 / US$12 each or HK$400 / US$50 for set of five.

Series: CERC Studies in Comparative Education

1. Mark Bray & W.O. Lee (eds.) (2001): *Education and Political Transition: Themes and Experiences in East Asia.* Second edition. ISBN 962-8093-84-3. 228pp. HK$200 / US$32.

2. Mark Bray & W.O. Lee (eds.) (1997): *Education and Political Transition: Implications of Hong Kong's Change of Sovereignty.* ISBN 962-8093-90-8. 169pp. (Out of print)

3. Philip G. Altbach (1998): *Comparative Higher Education: Knowledge, the University, and Development.* ISBN 962-8093-88-6. 312pp. HK$180 / US$30.

4. Zhang Weiyuan (1998): *Young People and Careers: A Comparative Study of Careers Guidance in Hong Kong, Shanghai and Edinburgh.* ISBN 962-8093-89-4. 160pp. HK$180 / US$30.

5. Harold Noah & Max A. Eckstein (1998): *Doing Comparative Education: Three Decades of Collaboration.* ISBN 962-8093-87-8. 356pp. HK$250 / US$38.

6. T. Neville Postlethwaite (1999): *International Studies of Educational Achievement: Methodological Issues.* ISBN 962-8093-86-X. 86pp. HK$100 / US$20.

7. Mark Bray & Ramsey Koo (eds.) (2004): *Education and Society in Hong Kong and Macao: Comparative Perspectives on Continuity and Change.* Second edition. ISBN 962-8093-34-7. 323pp. HK$200 / US$32. (Also available in Chinese)

8. Thomas Clayton (2000): *Education and the Politics of Language: Hegemony and Pragmatism in Cambodia, 1979-1989.* ISBN 962-8093-83-5. 243pp. HK$200 / US$32.

9. Gu Mingyuan (2001): *Education in China and Abroad: Perspectives from a Lifetime in Comparative Education.* ISBN 962-8093-70-3. 260pp. HK$200 / US$32.

10. William K. Cummings, Maria Teresa Tatto & John Hawkins (eds.) (2001): *Values Education for Dynamic Societies: Individualism or Collectivism.* ISBN 962-8093-71-1. 312pp. HK$200 / US$32.

11. Ruth Hayhoe & Julia Pan (eds.) (2001): *Knowledge Across Cultures: A Contribution to Dialogue Among Civilizations.* ISBN 962-8093-73-8. 391pp. HK$250 / US$38.

12. Robert A. LeVine (2003): *Childhood Socialization: Comparative Studies of Parenting, Learning and Educational Change.* ISBN 962-8093-61-4. 299pp. HK$200 / US$32.

13. Mok Ka-Ho (ed.) (2003): *Centralization and Decentralization: Educational Reforms and Changing Governance in Chinese Societies.* ISBN 962-8093-58-4. 230pp. HK$200/ US$32.

14. W.O. Lee, David L. Grossman, Kerry J. Kennedy & Gregory P. Fairbrother (eds.) (2004): *Citizenship Education in Asia and the Pacific: Concepts and Issues.* ISBN 962-8093-59-2. 313pp. HK$200 / US$32.

15. Alan Rogers (2004): *Non-Formal Education: Flexible Schooling or Participatory Education?* ISBN 962-8093-30-4. 316pp. HK$200/ US$32.

16. Peter Ninnes & Meeri Hellstén (2005): *Internationalizing Higher Education: Critical Explorations of Pedagogy and Policy.* ISBN 962-8093-37-1. 231pp. HK$200 / US$32.

17. Ruth Hayhoe (2006): *Portraits of Influential Chinese Educators.* ISBN 962-8093-40-1. HK$250 / US$38.

18. Aaron Benavot and Cecilia Braslavsky (eds.) (2006): *School Curricula for Global Citizenship: Comparative and Historical Perspectives on Educational Contents.* ISBN 962-8093-52-5. HK$200 / US$32.

Other books published by CERC

1. Mark Bray & R. Murray Thomas (eds.) (1998): *Financing of Education in Indonesia*. ISBN 971-561-172-9. 133pp. HK$140 / US$20.

2. Ruth Hayhoe (1999): *China's Universities 1895-1995: A Century of Cultural Conflict*. ISBN 962-8093-81-9. 299pp. HK$200 / US$32.

3. David A. Watkins & John B. Biggs (eds.) (2001): *Teaching the Chinese Learner: Psychological and Pedagogical Perspectives*. ISBN 962-8093-72-X. 306pp. HK$200 / US$32.

4. Mark Bray with Roy Butler, Philip Hui, Ora Kwo & Emily Mang (2002): *Higher Education in Macau: Growth and Strategic Development*. ISBN 962-8093-60-6. 127pp. HK$150 / US$24.

5. Yoko Yamato & Sally Course (2002): *Guide to International Schools in Hong Kong*. ISBN 962-8093-62-2. 82pp. HK$72 / US$12.

6. Ruth Hayhoe (2004): *Full Circle: A Life with Hong Kong and China*. ISBN 962-8093-31-2. 261pp. HK$200 / US$32.

7. David A. Watkins & John B. Biggs (eds.) (1996, reprinted 1999 & 2005): *The Chinese Learner: Cultural, Psychological and Contextual Influences*. ISBN 0-86431-182-6. 285pp. HK$200 / US$32.

8. Mark Bray & Ramsey Koo (eds.) (2005): *Education and Society in Hong Kong and Macao: Comparative Perspectives on Continuity and Change*. Second edition. ISBN 957-496-478-7. 318pp. HK$200 / US$32. (in Chinese)

9. Edward Vickers (2005): *In Search of an Identity: The Politics of History as a School Subject in Hong Kong, 1960s-2005*. ISBN 962-8093-38-X. 334pp. HK$200 / US$32.

Order through bookstores or from:

Comparative Education Research Centre
Faculty of Education
The University of Hong Kong
Pokfulam Road
Hong Kong
China

Fax: (852) 2517 4737
E-mail: cerc@hkusub.hku.hk
Website: www.hku.hk/cerc

The list prices above are applicable for order from CERC, and include sea mail postage; add US$10 for 1st copy for air mail; US$18 for the 2nd to 3rd copies; and US$40 for the 4th to 8th copies. For air mail order exceeding 8 copies, please contact CERC for exact amount.